Robert Salijeni

FINDING YOU

AMIDST

How to Question Everything, Learn Continuously
and Hustle Hard to Achieve Your Dream

CHAOS

Editor: Sonia Soneni Dube
Cover Design & Illustrations by Motsanaphe Morare
Published by The Golden Goose Institute (Pty)Ltd

Library of National Archives of Malawi-in-Publication Data is available

ISBN (Original): 978-999-080-8391

REVIEWS

Why should anyone buy or read this book?

This book will literally blow your mind. As Robert navigates through his personal experiences and shares without reservations various sources of inspiration, you will have no choice but to embark on your own journey of self-discovery.

—Dercio Mariote
Translator, Interpreter, Teacher.

Apart from the plethora of golden nuggets, for anyone looking to steer their life from the inside out, is the vulnerability he shares. Power is in the personal stories that Robert shares and his introspection of them. Well done Robert, the world is a better place because of your book.

—Grant Senzani
Author, Authors' Coach, Distinguished Toastmaster, Professional Speaker.

Insightful content shared through Robert's personal experiences in his quest to find his purpose. A relatable book that draws you in and allows you to embark on your own personal journey.

—Linda Chimanikire
Distinguished Toastmaster, Life Coach.

DEDICATION

My beloved parents, late dad, Joakim and mum, Annie.

You taught me the value of continuous learning and connections with others.

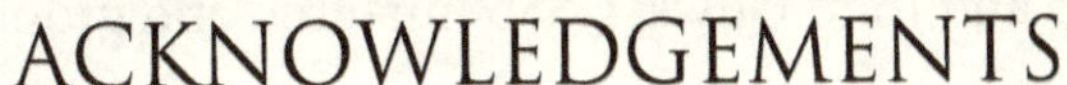

ACKNOWLEDGEMENTS

Special thanks go to all the people I have had the opportunity to interact with in my journey of life.

The first and most of all to receive these special thanks is Grant Senzani, a man, having met him for the first time, told him my story, believed in me. He worked relentlessly with me to make my dream of writing this book a reality. From the word – go, you read every chapter I wrote, word-for-word, and suggested the necessary changes to make this book what it is. To you, Grant, all I can say is, you are a true leader and inspirer, you have all it takes for any one to unleash their hidden dreams.

My beloved wife, Sekani Tamanda Salijeni, you did challenge and support me during this journey. You were my shoulder to lean on and still are. Thank you very much my darling wife.

Our beloved children, Annie, Augustine, Angel and Amy, you are great in your own way. Not only did we, together, craft the book title and subtitle, we also coined and polished the acronym – PAUSE. You are my greatest little helpers and creative team. You, guys have been awesome in every way possible to make this dream come true. I do cherish and value your company.

To experience and cherish life to the full, a lot of people especially my teachers through my school life, Mr. Lawrence Phuka and Mr L Nawena, inculcated sense and an inquisitive spirit in me; and my mentors, Mr. McChancy Mkamanga, late Bishop Patricia Pindeni, Ato Afful, Guy Dennison, Chimwemwe Luwani, Andy Harrington, Bert Jukes, Les Brown and Reverend Fathers, João Luis Dimba, CSSp and John Guwa, CSSp nurtured and groomed me.

The reviewers of this, Aletta Rochat, Arthur Thomas Ware, Atupele Ellah Stambuli, Dercio Donaldo Mariote, Emmanuel Chinunda, Grant Senzani, Linda Chimanikire, Luyanda Dlamini, Marco Jacobs and Veli Ndada, set aside their most precious time to read this book word-for-word and shared with me their insights to make it professional. I owe you all a lot for the role you played. You are my God given friends; you are forever close to my heart. Thank you very much.

It would be a disservice of me if I cannot appreciate Kain Ramsay, the coach who took me through NLP Practitioner and NLP Master Practitioner courses learning, who tirelessly drilled me to change the way I perceive and understand the people around me, the world and myself. He taught me to live a centred life, a life of purpose and living it inside out.

Last but one, I owe this book to all my friends, siblings, relatives and everyone whose interest is to live life to the full by living a purposeful life having had time to discover themselves.

Finally thank you very much God, the Almighty Father, for inspiring me to write, complete and publish this piece of work.

FOREWORD

B ob Salijeni's book, *Finding You amidst Chaos*, will certainly help many people, from all occupations, to understand clearly the importance of self-discovery, self-acceptance and self-mastery needed for pursuing one's purpose and destiny from the vantage point, a well-grounded knowledge of both one's strengths and weaknesses. Bob has wisely and artistically delivered on his promise of wanting to instill in the reader "the hunger to find the real you." He has done so by skillfully blending personal experience with his wide reading of other authors and lessons learnt from his role models, mentors and coaches. The work reveals the well-seasoned, selfless leader that Bob has become with the help of others, personal effort and grace.

One can confidently tell that Bob is not an amateur philosopher, a person only adept in theory. It is clear that he has walked on the road less travelled of self-discovery, self-acceptance and self-mastery. Consequently, he successfully discovered his life purpose and keenly employed the necessary discipline, values and goals in order to achieve that purpose. Hence, he advises us "Establishing an individual's values helps them to better understand themselves, their feelings and also gives them clarity relating to their future direction."

His writing style, which comes across as a fascinating conversation between himself and the reader is not only unique and captivating but also a very powerful and profound way of using personal experience to enrich the reader in a very gentle and yet convincing and compelling way. Right from the very beginning of the book to the end one realizes that Bob has walked the talk; has actualized himself and has truly led an effective life.

As one reads this book, it is unmistakably easy to see that Bob's quest for writing *Finding You amidst Chaos* is to help others become the best of themselves. Self-actualization, personal effectiveness and independence did not satisfy Bob. This man has refused to be caught up by what John C. Maxwell calls destination syndrome. Instead, he has chosen to transcend beyond success and multiply goodness, mentor one and all and to move from independence to inter-dependence and shift from effectiveness to greatness. No doubt, this writer is resolute to follow the footsteps of his leadership gurus that include his parents (Joakim and Annie), his beautiful and diligent wife (Sekani Tamanda), Kain Ramsay, Robin Sharma, Steve R. Covey, Oprah Winfrey, John C. Maxwell, Chiwoza Bandawe, Henry Kachaje, Nelson Mandela, Saint Mother Theresa of Calcutta, Myles Munroe and Popes Paul VI and Francis to mention but a few.

In this unique but obviously a "good read" book, Bob has weaved a real masterpiece work for motivating, inspiring and challenging the reader to live out their original selves through the discipline of valuing time, recognizing one's self-worth and assimi-lating proactive values and setting both short and long term goals in order to achieve greater purposes.

The diligent author gently and candidly shows the reader how thoughts, emotions, attitudes, beliefs, behaviors and habits affect personal, corporate and universal leadership. Anyone who will read this book will understand how important the questions that one asks about reality and life matter and define one's life. He clearly points out that our questions do play a great role in one's life, for better or for worse.

Conclusively, *Finding You amidst Chaos* will help the reader to maximize on better relationships and attitudes with self and other people. This work will help the reader to avoid the influence of small minded and negative people who may negatively influence the life decisions that one makes. The author did discover the beauty and importance of personal responsibility in personal development and the resilience needed for becoming the person intended by his or her Creator. Personal responsibility is much more than the influence of others, and it is the ultimate determinant in the pursuit of the original you amid the prevailing internal and the external noises or chaos. Bob, has come to the conclusion that in order for one to become the best version of themselves and in order for one to achieve one's singular life purpose, there is need not only for setting one's goals or identifying one's life purpose and hard work. The real big asset lies in one's ability and discipline to enjoy solitude which all great men and women, including the greatest religious leaders like Jesus of Nazareth, cherished. "They have had time to search within themselves to find the gifts they had. They had time to ask themselves important questions like who they were. What for were they here? What were their strengths and weaknesses? How could they use their strengths to contribute to the well-being of others in this world? Moreover, how could they improve and turn their weaknesses into fortes? This is how those men and women of valor found themselves. This is how they made it in life." Dear reader, take time to *Finding YOU amidst*

Chaos by valuing a pause because "Life without pausing is meaningless. A pause in life is very important. A pause helps us to step back and see ourselves in retrospective. A pause helps us see how far we have covered and how much further we intend to go to reach our destiny."

Reverend Father João Luis Dimba, CSSp

Roma - Italia

CONTENTS

WHY I WROTE THIS

Hello dear friend, and welcome to the beginning (or continuation) of your phenomenal life. Yes, by choosing to read this book, I do not doubt that your life will never be the same again. I believe that, should you commit to the words of this book, you will begin to live a marvelous life. I would like to start by saying thank you for spending your hard-earned money to purchase this book and for taking the time to embark on this journey of self-awareness with me. I know you really could be spending your time and money in other places so I do not take it lightly that you are flipping through this particular title.

I want you to know that I have written this book to instill in you the hunger to find the real you. You do not need to go through the life experiences I have gone through, but by you tapping into my experiences, you can discover yourself and live the true life you were meant to live. My hope with this book is to encourage you to stop wandering and continue living aimlessly, for your time is now. If you lose this moment, you might regret it later.

Have you found that you experience fleeting moments of joy and contentment in your life? Even then, these moments do not always feel like pure joy. Are your days overwhelmingly heavy and difficult to get through? Do you long for much more than the life you're currently living? Are you tired of wandering through life, unsure of who you really are and why you exist? Well then, I am glad you picked up this book because helping you answer these questions is why I wrote it.

To find the answers to these questions and to discover myself, I had to embark on a journey. A journey of continuous personal discovery and development where I chose to read a lot of books; books I never read at school, but ones that made me live life inside out. These are philosophical books. Glued to these books of philosophy, I came to know that only people who are guided by a philosophy of life manage to live a good life. Without a philosophy of life, you are like an individual who is at sea sailing without a compass - you will definitely get nowhere.

In order to get you started on your own journey, I want us to take a closer look at what life philosophies are and those that exist. In his book titled, ***A Guide to the Good Life: The Ancient Art of Stoic Joy***, William B Irvine states that whatever philosophy of life a person ends up adopting, s/he will probably have a better life than if s/he tried to live – as many people do – without a coherent philosophy. There are several branches of philosophy and some of them are Epicureanism, Cynicism, Hedonism, Skepticism, Stoicism and Zen Buddhism.

In her book titled, ***The Handy Philosophy Answer Book***, Naomi Zack (Ph.D.), takes time to shed more light on four different branches of philosophy except for Hedonism and Zen Buddhism. Here is what she says about these "four in brief":

- Epicureanism – Epicurean ethics held that pleasure is our only good; it is better even than virtue. Pain is only evil and so pleasure should be sought in stable ways, which makes a simple life necessary. The belief is that we should satisfy only our most necessary desires in the company of friends like us. Our ultimate goal should therefore be the absence of pain via a simple life for the body and the study of physics for the soul. This will result in *ataraxia*, or "freedom from disturbance."

- Cynicism – The cynics were eccentrics who chose to be outcasts rather than *kow-tow* to social norms that did not make sense to them. Ancient cynicism was generally an attempt to reassert the importance of human nature as independent of society and custom. Diogenes of Sinope thought people could learn much from dogs, who were not ashamed of their bodily functions, not picky eaters, and did not care where they slept.

- Skepticism – The skeptics held that nothing could be known, and they preached *epoce*, which is the doctrine that all judgements, conclusions, or assessments should be suspended. These academic skeptics posed problems, or *tropes*, to show that sensory knowledge is prone to error and reasoning does result in certainty. They concluded that because we have no absolute standards for distinguishing between truth and falsehood, the best way we can hope for is probable knowledge.

- Stoicism – Early stoic ethics held that only virtue (known as tranquility by Roman stoics) is good, and only vice is bad. Other things, such as health or wealth, may be preferred, but they are morally indifferent. We each have a unique role in the world and our job is to learn what it is. Such learning creates concern for the self, which can and should be extended to close relatives and friends and, after them, all humanity.

In his book titled ***Philosophy 101: From Plato and Socrates to Ethics and Metaphysics, an Essential Primer on the History of Thought***, Paul Kleinman states that "the term *hedonism* actually refers to several theories that, while different from one another, all share the same underlying notion: pleasure and pain are the only important elements of the specific phenomena the theories describe. In philosophy, hedonism is often discussed as a theory of value. This means that pleasure is the only thing intrinsically valuable to a person at all times and pain is the only thing intrinsically invaluable to an individual. Cyrenaics, in other words, were hedonists who believed that pleasure, specifically physical pleasure over mental pleasure, was the ultimate good and that immediate gratification was more desirable than having to wait for a long time for pleasure."

DT Suzuki wrote in the book, **An Introduction to Zen Buddhism**, that "Zen teaches nothing. Whatever teachings there are in Zen, they come out of one's mind. We teach ourselves; Zen merely points the way. Unless this pointing is teaching, there is certainly nothing in Zen purposely set up as its cardinal doctrines or as its fundamental philosophy." He further states that "Zen purposes to discipline the mind itself, to make it its own master, through an insight into its proper nature. This getting into the real nature of one's own mind or soul is the fundamental object of Zen Buddhism."

Of these branches of philosophy, I fell in love with Stoicism. Why? It's a type of philosophy that helps me to live life inside out. What intrigued me was that in this book, William B Irvine states that when he read the works of the Stoics, he encountered individuals who were cheerful and optimistic about life (even though they made it a point to spend time thinking about all the bad things that could happen to them) and who were fully capable of enjoying life's pleasures (while at the same time being careful not to be enslaved by those pleasures). He also encounters, much to his surprise, individuals who valued joy; indeed, according to Seneca, what Stoics seek to discover 'is how the mind may always pursue a steady and favorable course, may be well-disposed towards itself, and may view its conditions with joy.' He further states that Seneca asserts that someone who practices Stoic principles 'must, whether he wills or not, necessarily be attended by constant cheerfulness and a joy that is deep and issues from deep within, since he finds delight in his own resources, and desires no joys greater than his inner joys.'

We can only live our life to the fullest the moment we realize that within us is all we need to lead a good life. I found the meaning of my existence having spent quality time understanding Stoicism.

Whatever we seek outside us brings with it, sadness and pain. The more reason you and I need to spare time for ourselves to engage in introspection to find ourselves. Having understood the importance of having a life philosophy, the next question to tackle would be how you can find yourself.

1. Take a Personal Strengths and Weaknesses Assessment

Through my experiences and interactions with various people in life, I have managed to find myself. This was done after a thorough strengths and weaknesses analysis. I had to find time to myself and challenge myself by engaging in an honest debate with myself. I looked within in order to do an honest self-assessment. Through this frank assessment, I discovered my strengths and weaknesses. I came to know that I am a confident, persistent and vivacious person. I also came to realize that I am very good at speaking to people, whether one on one or in public; comfortable and at ease with making friends with people I meet for the first time; I am down to earth and have very good leadership skills. On the other hand, I came to find out that I have a short temper and I tend to speak whatever comes to my mind without thinking about the effects on the people I am responding to. I also noted that sometimes I am a procrastinator, and I want to work at my own pace.

With the knowledge gained from this assessment, I had to tame my anger and cultivate my listening skills, ensuring that I built strong relationships with people. I learned to start journaling, which in the end helped me with my procrastination by writing down in advance what I intended on doing the next day. I also learned to major in minor things like Andy Harrington said. Concentrating on a few projects with maximum attention and giving these my very best attention. It is imperative that you learn to put all your energy on two or three important tasks a day and do these three tasks very well one at a time. Great results can only be realized if we concentrate our attention on one task at a time unlike doing too many things at the same time that result in zero productivity.

What are your strengths and weaknesses? How are you going to turn your weaknesses into strengths? Now spare some time alone responding to these two questions.

2.   Discover Your Passion

My personal assessment helped me in finding my passion. My passion is public speaking and leadership. With this discovery, I joined Toastmasters International to perfect my speaking and leadership skills. While working on these two skills I have learned to speak professionally and develop as a leader, active listening has been one of the skills I have acquired that I initially paid little attention to. You can never be a great leader unless you learn to be a good listener and pay attention to what others are saying. More often than not, we tend to hear what others are saying with ready answers in our minds, ready to respond as soon as they are done speaking. That is not what true leadership is all about.

But why am I working towards improving my skills? I am interested in becoming one of the best in the world, offering people unique skillsets that will make them better through self-discovery. Having discovered themselves, they can then put their passion to good use in order to impact other people's lives.

What are you passionate about? Ever thought of this? And what skills are you interested in acquiring to make you one of the best in the world? Find time to discover your passion by answering these questions.

3. Use Your Passion for a Good Cause

Being a professional speaker, I learned that I am a teacher. Speaking to people allows me to impart some unique knowledge and skills that, once put to good use, can empower them to live their lives to the full. I am already coaching and mentoring young entrepreneurs to manage their businesses well, valuing connections, tapping into new knowledge through continuous personal development and living life from the inside out.

There are people out there who are hopeless and clueless. There are people out there who are less privileged. These people need someone to reach them. They need someone who can talk to them and give them hope. They need someone who can share with them skills to help them unleash their potential and become the best of themselves. I am willing to give these people a hand. I am prepared to take them through skills training that will make them fulfill their dreams.

With my passion, I want to reach out to as many needy young men and women who are pursuing their education but have no one to assist them. Where ever possible I intend to pay for their school fees and assist them in thinking and acting differently. These young men and women are used to a certain lifestyle, and education comes with new experiences. These new experiences can be strange to these young men and women, and preparing them to meet and absorb them is imperative. This way they can reach their dreams and live a fulfilled life.

How do you intend to use your passion? What do you want people to write on your tombstone? How do you want to be remembered? Life is about leaving a legacy. What will yours be? Think about these questions and answer them as truthfully as you can.

"It's hard to beat a person who never gives up," stated Babe Ruth. You are created to find the original you. To live your life inside out, you need to get to know who you really are. You need to know both your strengths and weaknesses. But that is not all, you also need to discover what you are really good at, and having realized your passion, put it to great use. You can only live your life inside out if you are fully aware of yourself.

Finally, remember that each one of us is unique. With this uniqueness, we are endowed with different gifts. We must take the initiative to find out what these gifts are that we've been given in order to help us live a life of purpose, a life of contribution and a life of making a difference in other people's existence. To realize our purpose, we need to PAUSE so as to find ourselves amidst chaos. Chaos, in this case, implies our lack of attention to oneself because we are blinded by recklessness, negativity, lack of faith, fear and digital noise through social media.

Chapter One

MY LIFE AT A GLANCE

"Problems are like washing machines.
They twist, they spin and knock us around.
But in the end, we come out cleaner, brighter and
better than before."
- Unknown

Every story begins somewhere. I want you to know where I came from, what I have had to overcome and where I am right now. This is in hopes that my story will encourage you and spark a flame within you to journey on in discovering your true self.

My Initial Dreams

Like any good story, it all starts with one beautiful sunny day.

While still a little boy, 11 years old, I woke up with a dream. A dream of becoming a mechanical engineer. What a huge fantasy for a little boy then. Certainly crazy and laughable wouldn't you say? Would you like to know why I wanted to become an engineer? Hang on, and get ready to laugh!

As a child, I was fascinated by truck drivers. Our village, Chimbalame Village, in Mchinji (which is on the Western border between Malawi and Zambia), endowed with a dense forest of natural trees and fertile arable soil, and a variety of natural fruits during the rainy season, is a stone's throw away from the main road. Not only is our village endowed with a dense forest, it also has a stretch of grassland that looks amazingly beautiful during the rainy season. It was during the rainy season, when fruits were in abundance, that I would go to the road and spend the day there selling either bananas or mangoes.

It was on one of those days that I became interested in the trucks that were passing by. One of these trucks stopped nearby, and the driver got out to ask me the price of the mangoes I was selling. I found myself breathless the moment he pulled out cash from his pocket to pay for a full bucket of mangoes! When I reached home, I crumped to the floor and found myself in a reverie, thinking deeply about the noble job those drivers did. Thoughts of their sacrifice, at the expense of quality time with their families, blew my mind. I looked at them as my greatest heroes: I admired how they sacrificed their lives serving others.

While on a holiday at another time, I saw one stationary truck. Its driver had come to deliver relief food to Mozambican refugees at a border village between Malawi and Mozambique, in Mchinji. This further piqued my interest in becoming a truck driver. In addition to this, it crossed my mind that were I to become a truck driver, I would want to repair my truck myself should I face a breakdown on one of my errands. This was the reason why I wanted to become a mechanical engineer. All this in the process of serving people.

Fast forward a few years, and these dreams would soon be forgotten as I moved to the village, which was the result of a mishap. It began with the harsh reality of my dear parents separating after being together for eleven years, and my mother heading for her village with my three sisters. That was in 1979 when I was seven years old. I was left in town with my father. It did not only rain on me, but it poured heavily on me from that point on. My father brought in a step mother who did not like me at all. She used to nag him and gave him sleepless nights because she did not want me to stay with them. My father tried to reason with her that he wanted to raise and groom his only son himself, but this did not please her. Every night was a nightmare for my father. In the end he had no option but to vie for the best decision - to succumb to her wishes for his peace and the safety of his only son.

After staying with my father and step mother for one year, my father began fearing for my well-being. He took me to my mother in the village and left me there, all this in the effort to save the life of his only son.

Life in the Village

A new chapter of life began in the village that was not all that much better than the one I had left. My mother's kinsmen had never liked us and since we had lived the former part of our lives in town, they rebelled against us. We were told to our faces, 'You had fun in town, now it's your turn to suffer and feel what it is to be in the village'. It turned out to be hell on earth indeed. There were days when my mother would have nothing for us to eat, and after asking for help from her relatives none would give her a hand. In such instances, we ended up sleeping on empty stomachs.

My mother worked hard in the field, cultivating to raise four children on her own. This was great as she was an encourager and motivator to us all. She did, and still does, value education. She toiled to ensure that all four of us went to school. It was exciting attending school, and the long-distance walks to school started building a strong character in me.

One day, while back from school and thinking of all the pain I was going through together with my siblings, I told myself this: 'I don't belong here, I shall return where I came from'. My mother's hard-working spirit and independent personality did not deserve the negativity we received from our mother's kinsmen.

For instance, my uncle used to call me all sorts of names and would deride me saying things along the lines of: "You useless and spoilt chap! You will never achieve anything tangible in life!" Or, "You are the worst child among all the nephews I have!" His behavior would often raise my temper and created a voice inside me that urged me to prove him wrong. This raised lots of energy and courage within me. Thus, it resulted in me becoming the star at my primary school and my newfound fame had everyone talking about me.

Life at Seminary

I excelled and in no time, found myself at St Kizito Seminary in Dedza. This secondary school is for young men who are interested in becoming priests. While here, I and my fellow classmates were bullied heavily. We were beaten and mocked in every manner you can think of. Just imagine cold water being poured on you while in the comfort of your bed still asleep dreaming, or suddenly being woken up by slaps to your face. How would you have felt? This experience brought out a fighter in me. Having endured all that bullying, I came out strong and persistent. I kept focused on my goal: to become a mechanical engineer. I worked hard and was always scooping amazing grades in class. I am not perfect, however, because regardless of my results I finished my secondary school life on a bad note.

I was expelled from the seminary for misbehaving. I failed to attend morning prayers one day and instead led a group of young men to the school's garden to uproot the school's cassava and sugarcane. This was a decision birthed from receiving rice porridge without sugar and milk that particular morning. Such actions resulted in me having to walk from the nearby village to write my final examinations. This brought pain and broke my mother's heart who saw me as a priest in future.

The results came and despite being expelled, I got great results.

Tertiary Education and its Experiences

One night while home in the village, I was chatting and having fun with my siblings and extended family. The radio was on and I heard the announcer start to share the names of those students who had made it into the University of Malawi.

I became curious and so did my family. If you were there that night you would have seen all ears glued to the radio. Amongst the list announced my name was mentioned. I was selected to pursue a Bachelor of Business Studies program at The Polytechnic!

I jumped up, clasping my hands to my chest and screamed, "Yes! Yes! Yes!" I ran home to tell my mother the great news. My mother was excited, and she started dancing. All her anger against me evaporated instantly.

While jubilant, my cousin came and said, "Eish, my bad Robert, how come? You heard the announcer wrongly. It was Rose Salijeni from Stella Maris Secondary School who had been selected." My mum and I kept quiet but after she had left, I assured my mother that it was my name that I heard.

In the morning, I went to a trading center and managed to get a newspaper for the weekend, Malawi News. Perusing through the paper, I came across the list of the students' names who had been selected to go to the University of Malawi, and my name was there. I was vindicated! I bought it and went home more excited than before to show my mother. My cousin, even though the previous night she had insisted that I was not mentioned during the announcements, congratulated me.

Mechanical Engineering?

The dream of becoming a mechanical engineer never came true. My interests had now changed and the level of insight I had about myself as well had increased. I felt I was a people's person and needed to pursue a course that would allow me to interact well with people all the time.

I obtained a Bachelor of Business Administration degree through the University of Malawi. After the completion of my studies, I saw what a hassle it was to find a job. I sent letters of application to various companies; I even visited various companies and presented my case, but nothing fruitful came from that. I became frustrated and started questioning the essence of education.

Then an idea came to mind one day while I was home chatting with my cousins. I decided that I would visit a colleague of my father, Mr. Ian Khanje, who had his own company called United Freight Forwarders Limited to ask him for a job.

He received me well and we chatted. During our chat he asked me why I came to see him. I told him the reason and he said that he had no vacancy for me. I stared straight into his eyes and pleaded with him for a job but he insisted, telling me that there was no place for me. He then told me to get out of his office since he wanted to concentrate on his work, and I responded, "I am not leaving this office until you offer me a job." He rose from his chair and glared at me with anger shouting, 'I say get out of my office now!'

After he saw that it was a lost case, he sat down and concentrated on his work. Some time passed and then he stared at me again and said, "Young man, don't you listen? Get out of my office now! Do you want me to call security?" I once again looked at him, still at ease, and said I was not going anywhere until he gave me my job.

Lunch hour came. He wanted to leave his office for lunch and asked me to go. I told him that I would not leave until he gave me the job. He then looked me straight in the eyes again and said, "Alright I will offer you a job. Come tomorrow to get started, but I won't be paying you." I accepted the offer and the next day I was hired as a Sales Officer. I was exhiralated to have finally got the job. Every day I looked forward to going back to work since this was my first experience of work. I learnt a lot from the team I was working with and this made my work life simple.

Within three months of starting that job, I was invited to an interview at another company called Enterprise Containers Limited, a subsidiary of Press Corporation. There were 30 of us that applied and the company was only looking for one person. I ended up being selected out of the 30 and went on to the second interview. After the second interview, I received an offer for the job. I was exhilarated with my accomplishment, having been chosen out of a pool of 30 people!

My initial job title at this company was Management Trainee. After I had successfully completed my probationary period, I was made a Sales Officer and my job included being responsible for a large sales force and several warehouse teams. I enjoyed it!

Nine months down the line, I was promoted to Marketing Manager. This was a recommendation made by my former boss who was leaving for another company. I took over from him. I became a peoples' person, just as I had wanted because with this job, I got to interact with a lot of customers, both individuals and corporates. Serving and satisfying the needs of these customers left me feeling ecstatic.

Time to Get Married

While working as a Marketing Manager, I finally tied the knot with my closest friend, Prisca Mkandawire, a beautiful lady I had courted for six years. I was staying with my uncle during the holidays in town while studying at The Polytechnic. Early one morning, as I was coming from church that is when I met her. Here she was, facing me, a beautiful and irresistible young lady, smiling and vivacious. I greeted her and after a little chitchat, we parted ways. It's her ever-smiling demeanor and vitality that drew me to her.

For our honeymoon, we went to Chikale Beach, Nkhata Bay, a unique and beautiful beach resort along the northern part of Malawi. Great moments were shared; from the evening dinners by candlelight on clear sandy beaches with romantic music in the background; to swimming in the lake. After such a blissful time we went back to our home in Newlands, Blantyre.

Little did I know that 28 days after our marriage, I would lose my darling wife. We were on our way to attend my cousin's wedding in Lilongwe, which is 312 km from Blantyre. We started off early in the morning around 05:30 hours, enjoying our drive with beautiful Craig David songs playing in the background. Along the way, our car, a red Nissan 4 x 4 Hardbody, suddenly jolted to my left and overturned three times.

My dear wife, Prisca, not having buckled up, was thrown out of the car as it was overturning. I remained in the car until it came to rest. My seat belt protected me. I was pulled out of the car with a broken right arm.

We were taken to the nearest hospital, Dedza District Hospital. My dear wife was taken straight into the ICU while I was taken into the operating theatre for an operation on my right arm. My operation was haphazardly done, and to make matters worse, it was really cold and I was given no blankets. I ended up shivering a lot and could not sleep as a result.

While in that state, around 17:00 hours, I overheard some nurses whispering that my wife was no more. I was speechless. I abruptly rose from the bed and told them that I wanted to see my wife with tears rolling down my cheeks.

The two nurses overpowered me and forced me to lie back on the bed. In the process, I slept while in pain. Around 23:00 hours, I was driven back to Blantyre at Mwaiwathu Private Hospital where I ended up in theatre for the second time. Dr. Devor Kumipongera had to operate on my right hand again. He did a great job, and a hand that was supposed to be amputated was brought back to life. I salute this man for his craftsmanship and his attention to detail.

Most of my body was heavily bruised during the accident and my head was partly affected. After the second successful operation, I came out of the theatre unconscious and in a coma. My dear wife, on the other hand, was buried in our home village cemetery while I was in a coma.

I was discharged from the hospital and went home to Newlands, Chigumula. While there, and having lost my memory from being in a coma, I thought my dear wife had gone away for some time and would be back. As a result, one day I called my cousin, Mike Ketulo, to tell me the whereabouts of my wife. He told me that he was coming home since he could not tell me over the phone.

He came home and we started chatting. During our chat, he asked me what I had said to him on the phone. I repeated the question, "Where is my wife and when is she coming back? I don't remember her saying bye to me." He stared at me and shook his head. Then, finally he spilt the beans: "Your wife is no more. You were involved in a car accident and you lost her then." I started crying uncontrollably. He allowed me to cry and later on advised me to take courage.

Questions started rushing into my head and no answers could be found. Questions like: why did God allow this to happen to me? How could God only allow me to have short-lived happiness? Is He really a God that loves His people? I found myself at a loss. Frustrated and boiling with fury, I made a resolution that I would never marry again.

I went to Thunga Parish in Thyolo to ask for answers from priests who were my close friends and they told me they had no answers for my difficult questions. Eventually, they told me never to visit them again if I would continue to ask such questions.

Suicidal thoughts followed. I came to the conclusion that there was no reason to live. One night, I called Father John Dimba and asked him what happens to people who commit suicide. He asked me – 'Do you want to commit suicide, Robert?' I answered him – 'No'. Yet, deep inside I had made up my mind to kill myself. We had a deep conversation, and I eventually slept while talking with him. Early in the morning, the next day, he called me and asked me – 'Robert, are you alive?' I answered him – 'Yes'. He told me to see him immediately after breakfast.

I went to see him and eventually he took me through a counseling session. This was the first of a number of counseling sessions he had set up for me. He told me that while I was asking God, "Why me?" I should have been asking God, "Why not me?" He proceeded to tell me that I was saved from the accident for a reason, and it was this reason that I was to look for.

He further said, "Imagine, how many people you would affect by killing yourself?" I was astounded by that question and responded, "What do you mean by that?" He said "You have your parents, sisters and relatives who look up to you for support. If you kill yourself, then you will kill them since they will have no one to offer them support. Think about it. Be wise young man, thank God you are alive and find out from Him why He spared you". That conversation opened up my mind and I saw the world from a different perspective. It's this great man, Father Dimba, who saved me from taking my life.

Life After the Tragedy

I continued my work as Marketing Manager serving people as usual, but eventually found no joy in the job as it did not challenge me any longer. I felt the work was routine. Frustration kicked in and all the vigor in me vanished. I am an individual who loves challenges. Facing challenges and overcoming them is what keeps me going. It was in those moments of frustration that I told myself, "Young man quit this job - there is no room for growth for you anymore." I left a few days later in search of a real challenge.

A month down the line, I got another job as Client Service Executive at an advertising agency. I instantly fell in love with the job; it had lots of challenges. Every project I managed for my clients offered a new challenge altogether, and these challenges developed within me a sense of satisfaction. No longer was my work routine, and by the end of each day I found myself happy and satisfied that I had served my clients well. I also enjoyed exceeding their expectations.

At the end of my first year with this company, I fell in love with a beautiful and pacific lady called Sekani Tamanda Ndasauka who was a fellow workmate. Our relationship blossomed and our love and passion for one another intensified. As a result, the time came for us to marry and on 31st December 2005, Sekani and I tied the knot.

She then stopped working because we experienced challenges at work with our boss around our relationship. I carried on with work, nonetheless, and life continued to progress wonderfully. In November 2006, we had our first-born daughter, Annie Fortune Salijeni. Not only were Sekani and I blessed with Annie Fortune, but God also blessed us with Augustine Favour, our only son in June 2008; then two other daughters, Angel Faith in September 2010 and Amy Feodora in December 2012. This is my elite support crew that energizes me to always look at each new day with positive energy.

In terms of my career, I was later promoted to Senior Account Director. Everything was going on superbly well for me. The challenges I encountered every day during this period made me fall in love with my job. I was operating at the highest level and this went on for five years.

Nelly Furtado sang a song titled *All Good Things (Come to an End)*. Indeed, the time soon came for me to leave. I had worked for five years without a holiday and felt that I would break down at any moment. I needed fresh air to rejuvenate myself. Eventually, a day came and I told myself, "Young man, it's time to quit this job." Something in me told me that it was time I started something new of my own.

Entrepreneurship

Because of the great and amazing relationships I had built with people; and the encouragement and support from my closest companion and darling wife, Sekani, I was able to start my own company. This courageous decision also left me as the laughing stock of my colleagues with whom I attended university. They laughed at me because I was now walking to work.

You see, I had resigned from a job with lots of benefits including a company car, medical scheme and house rentals paid for by the company, to mention a few. Now, I was on my own covering long distance trips from home to work, and back home again every day. I was labeled mad since I had chosen to leave a good job for the option of starting my own business.

I endured pain in my legs as I walked long distances each day and spent my lunch hours without food. It was in those moments, however, that I grew a tough skin, became courageous and persevered. Life became great again for me. A new adventure was on the horizon and I loved pondering every detail of what was to come next.

Embracing Challenges

Over time, my life changed. Three months down the line from starting the company, the media houses I was dealing with asked for their payments to be made or they would discontinue business with my company. While pondering my next move, I remembered that the company that had wanted to employ me had promised to support me financially if I found myself stuck along the way. I picked up the phone and called the CEO of this company, Ato Afful, and told him that I was stuck, and had no money. Guess what happened next? Instead of asking me why I wanted the money, he asked how much I needed. I told him that I needed K5 million, and the next day I had this money transferred into our company account. I paid up all the media houses and became the hero! From zero to hero. With contacts (connections), commitment, good relationships, passion, resilience, and synergy, I made my way into the advertising industry.

Challenges were embraced along the way. One such challenge came in 2009 when we had won a Zain account. This client was based in Lilongwe while our offices were in Blantyre. We were supposed to have weekly status meetings every Tuesday at 08:00 hours at their offices. This meant that I and the team working on this account had to travel to Lilongwe, 312 kms in distance, to attend the weekly status meetings. We would wake up at 03:00 hours and start off for Lilongwe by 04:00 hours, arriving by 07:30 hours. We would have a quick breakfast in Lilongwe before proceeding to meet our client for our status meeting. Having concluded our meeting, we would then leave for Blantyre around 13:00 hours in the afternoon to arrive in Blantyre around 17:00hours. This routine became a part of us, and carried on for three months. Eventually, we agreed to have these meetings through teleconferencing. Life during that period was not easy, but I saw this as my time to work hard and challenge my capabilities. Along the way, life has taught me great lessons; lessons never learned in class. I am now a mature individual because I have gone through the ups and downs of life with resilience and will power.

Conclusion

Looking at my life, it has been a life full of challenges and conquests. But looking critically at these conquests, these were achieved to please my bosses wherever I worked. I wanted to deliver beyond their expectations and that gave me a sense of satisfaction. Amidst this, however, I was also chasing the wind; I chose to look for happiness in things outside of me. Perhaps you can relate? For me, this was the reason I had been doing everything well. I thought me being the best student and best employee would equate to real happiness. However, it proved otherwise.

I lost steam after spending some time with each company I worked for. I ended up with frustrations and critical questions. Questions like, 'What are my strengths and weaknesses?' 'What is it that I am passionate about?' And, 'How can I use my passion for a good cause?' These questions never got their answers from the work I was doing. These questions required me to do some soul searching.

Have you done yours already? You might be frustrated like I had been. You might be going to work daily while deep inside, fire is burning and anger is boiling. You might be going through the frustration of not realizing your true self. Our true selves have and shall never be found in the work we do every day at our places of employment. Our true selves can be found within ourselves, after deep introspection. This personal assessment can lead us into the discovery of our strengths and weaknesses, finding out what our passions are, and setting out to put those passions to good use.

Your life and experiences might not be like mine. While some of us have gone through hell and came back alive and strong, others have had a smooth ride. All great men and women, however, were ordinary people who endured tough times and focused on their dreams. I want you to focus on your dreams, and push the excuses to the side. Regardless of how things may be at this present moment, I want you to know a better life awaits you.

To begin that better life, however, you need to find your purpose, which I did only in the latter parts of my life. You do not have to wait that long. You can do so now.

In the next chapter, you will come across the importance of finding your purpose as you embark on this journey of finding the real you in chaos. To get to this purpose you need to set up goals: these can be short, medium-, and long-term goals. As you pursue your life purpose while achieving your goals, you end up realizing your dreams. Turn to the next pages to learn more about the importance of finding your purpose and goal setting in enhancing your life.

Chapter Two

PURPOSE: WHAT IS YOURS AND WHAT DO YOU NEED IN ORDER TO ACHIEVE IT?

"Your life has purpose. Your story is important. Your dreams count. Your voice matters. You were born to make an impact."
– Unknown

No one grows in isolation. In fact, the Chewa of Malawi say, *"kalikokha nkanyama, tili tiwiri ntianthu"*, and the Zulus of South Africa say, *"umuntu ngumuntu ngabantu"*; both African proverbs mean that a person is a person because of the help of other people. In life, other people play a great role in us discovering ourselves and in shaping or molding us. We might think we know ourselves fully, yet we are clueless. I would like to encourage you to spare some time and go through whatever conversations you have had with the people in your life. Recalling these conversations and isolating lessons from them helps us discover who we really are and what we are here for.

The Power of Curiosity

It was one beautiful summer's morning in October while learning English in my primary school class, that our English teacher, Mr. Lawrence Phuka, boisterously uttered, "*He who does not know that he doesn't know, is not fit to live*". I, gazing with focus, pondered on this quote and then asked myself what it meant. I was baffled and did not get the answer.

During break time, I began reminiscing on the teacher's quote while chatting with my colleagues and asked them if they understood it. They shook their heads and unanimously said 'No!' Then I asked my colleagues why we did not pluck up enough courage to ask our teacher what he meant. Nobody said a thing.

The following day came and we found ourselves in an English class session, yet again, on a beautiful sunny day. The hour came when our English teacher asked us if we had any questions about what he had just taught us that day. We all responded that we had none; all was crystal clear. But I, exuding calm and focus, raised my hand and said, "Teacher, I have a question. Not to do with today's lesson though, but yesterdays." He, displaying a wide grin, responded, "Go ahead, and ask." Then I proceeded to ask him what he meant by the quote – '*He who does not know that he doesn't know, is not fit to live*.' He said to me, "Brilliant! I am moved by your probing question little boy". He then proceeded to graciously give us the meaning of the quotation.

He asserted that in life, most people are living aimlessly because of ignorance. He further expressed that ignorance makes most people wander about without fully understanding why they are living: they lead a purposeless life. In the end, they only exist and do not live. I, then said, 'You have puzzled us again.' 'What do you mean by existing and not living?' He said that there is a difference between existing and living: those people who live to satisfy their own needs and enjoy life aimlessly, only exist; while those who live a life that contributes to the well-being of others in one way or another, live.

He further challenged us that unless we came to realize why we are here on this planet, we shall never live a fulfilled life. He challenged us at that age to find out why we were going to school. Young as we were, we started thinking of why we were going to school. It was such a challenge from our English teacher that made me ask intelligent questions all the time.

Set Your Priorities Straight

Later on, I found myself in college with my peers where we enjoyed our newfound freedom. The freedom of choice: the choice of attending classes or not; the freedom of going to grab a beer, drinking like a fish, chilling out with women, or studying. Wow, it was a newfound joy! Little did we know that freedom comes with responsibility. We eventually learned the hard way when most of us had failed a certain course miserably. This gave us a rude awakening, and then we were forced to evaluate our choices and redefine our priorities.

We were enjoying a Business Law class session one cold and cloudy afternoon in June when our Business Law lecturer, Mr. L Nawena, gave us this quote – "*Where there is no vision, the people perish*". He went on to say, 'You, young men and women, do you know why you are here?' His question was borne out of the fact that some of our classmates had gone to bury the remains of our fellow student who was hit by a car on the road because he was drunk. His life was taken abruptly as a result of pursuing the wrong priorities.

He said, "Imagine how your friend has died; young and without realizing his dreams. Not only that, but he has also broken his parents' hearts as well." He went on to say, 'I want you all to remember this proverb – *where there is no vision, the people perish.* You are here for school and not for fun. You are here to realize your dreams and not to chase skirts.' Finally, he said, 'Find your why. Once you find it, pursue it relentlessly. Don't follow the crowd - stand on your own and stick to your guns.' We found ourselves quiet that day, absorbing our lecturer's message.

Find Yourself Through Others

On several occasions as I was growing up, relatives, friends, teachers, and workmates I interacted with told me that I shall be a great teacher one day. This honestly annoyed me a lot. I responded to them by saying that I was not interested in becoming a teacher. I had other interests in mind unlike that of teaching. Time went by, and still, after having conversations with friends and relatives, the same comments came through that I would turn into a wonderful teacher. This kept me wondering and asking myself the question – why? Try as I may, I never got answers to that question. I grew up and pursued marketing as a career. My career soared and I managed to reach *"great heights attained by great men, who while their friends were sleeping and snoring, were toiling upwards in the night"* (Henry Wadsworth Longfellow, paraphrased). I was the happiest man with my conquests. Nevertheless, what I accomplished did not lead me in finding my why.

Discover Yourself Through Your Experiences

In the process of ruminating over my why, I felt that I was born to do more than what I was grossly glued to doing – Marketing. I then told myself that the time had come to ponder my next move in life. While I was deep in such thoughts, my colleagues at work told me that I was gifted with confidence and that I needed to put it to good use. Whenever I was asked to make a presentation to a team of colleagues at work or to a client to sell an idea, it was always an effortless process and I would receive applauds for my effort. On many occasions, I found myself chosen as team leader whenever I attended conferences abroad with my colleagues. We would be divided into groups for discussions and would later on present our findings or proposal to the rest of the class, and in most cases, I ended up being chosen as the leader to present on behalf of the particular group I was a part of. This fascinated me. My presentation skills improved tremendously, and my confidence levels soared too. Remarks and feedback from colleagues made me realize that indeed, it was imperative that I find out how I could maximize my confidence.

Reap the Good from Social Media

It was on a particularly beautiful, cool and cloudy afternoon, while enjoying an amazingly cooked lunch of crocodile fillet and steamed white rice accompanied with a mouth-watering green salad at Protea Ryalls Hotel, that I saw a post on Facebook that intrigued me. It was a post by Henry Kachaje about the National Achievers Congress 2014 which was to take place in Midrand, South Africa. The way he praised this event, stating that it was for those entrepreneurs determined to grow in their pursuits and a must-attend conference, turned my attention off my great meal to read this post carefully. I took a screenshot of this post and proceeded to finish my lunch while sipping a glass of red wine from one of the rare choices of South African wines. It was one of the unique lunch breaks that I hold so dear and cannot forget.

Immediately when I got back to the office, I opened my laptop and searched for this particular event, National Achievers Congress 2014, and read up on the conference. Then, as usual, being an adventurous person, I called the inquiries number found at the bottom of the page, and learned a lot from the salesperson who answered; a gentleman who knew the event like the back of his hand and patiently attended to me while responding to my questions with respect and expertise. I then registered my colleague, Innocent Willinga, and I for the event.

Innocent and I flew South African Airways to Johannesburg very curious and as inquisitive as children. We stayed in Rosebank at the Courtyard Gardens. All this was done in an effort to learn from the great achievers of our time; men of valor and dreamers like Les Brown, Andy Harrington, JT Foxx, Peng Joon, Nick Vujicic, Robert Kiyosaki, T Harv Eker and many more.

The following morning, we were in a taxi to Midrand to start our new journey as entrepreneurs. At the conference, we met and interacted with many entrepreneurs from all walks of life. What a great and thrilling experience it was! One after another, these men shared their stories and great lessons were learned from them. They relayed their personal narratives, from the challenges they encountered to the successes they had achieved. They emphasized to us that nothing worth having comes easy. They also insisted that successful people make a lot of mistakes, but they don't quit. It is through toiling that we realize our dreams. They spoke of grinding and never giving up in life. We were astounded with the power of their messages, the eloquence of their presentation skills, and their expertise in the fields they were presenting. Moved by Les Brown's *'Power of Your Story'*, we registered with his team to learn and perfect our public speaking skills and learn from him.

These great achievers boggled our minds with immense knowledge never taught in school, for three consecutive days, and then it came to an end. The event, nevertheless, opened my mind and eventually led me to discover that I could do more than I thought I ever could. This experience left me with a hunger to dig deep into myself and find out why I was, and still am living. I wish you could have been there, and you would surely agree with me that the lessons were enormous and out of this world.

Continuously Keep Improving Yourself

It is Les Brown who opened my eyes further during this special conference that I attended which took place in Rosebank, South Africa at the Radisson Blue Hotel in March 2015, where only a chosen few were in attendance. During this conference, he drilled in us storytelling skills and encouraged us to share our stories. This is when I learned that I was a great storyteller. We were trained for two days and on the last day of this training session, Les Brown advised me to look for a Toastmasters International club in my country. He told me that my professional speaking skills would improve tremendously if only I joined this club. I knew little about Toastmasters International then but I was determined to discover more.

When I returned home, Blantyre, my search for a Toastmasters International club proved futile. I found none. Meanwhile, my hunger to learn the public speaking skill kept growing. This meant that I had my eyes wide open and was alert so that I would be ready when the opportunity availed itself.

Luckily, an opportunity did come up. My colleague, Levie Nkunika, had posted a Toastmasters International open event that was to take place at the Protea Ryalls Hotel, sometime in April 2015.

The post stated that those interested in attending the event should register online. I immediately registered!

Needless to say that on the day the event took place, I was in attendance. The proceedings were breathtaking and I enjoyed every moment of it. Many young men and women presented their speeches. They spoke about Toastmasters International, when it was established and why it exists. I found myself at home. I registered myself for Toastmasters International, and subsequently became a member of Eloquent Toastmasters Club.

Find Yourself a Mentor

Upon joining Eloquent Toastmasters Club, not only did my professional speaking improve, but I also learned leadership skills. I remember vividly when my mentor, Chimwemwe Luwani, drilled me as I was practicing my icebreaker - this is the first speech every Toastmaster makes upon joining a club.

Chimwemwe would set aside time for us to go through my speech as a practice run. During this time, he showed eagerness to hear me speak. While listening intently he timed my speech as well. Once I was done reciting my speech, he gave me feedback and shared areas I did well in and those that required improvement. We would go through this process again and again until he was convinced that I had incorporated his feedback.

The practice was great, and the lessons learned brilliant. You see, when you have someone to instruct you on how you can learn a new skill and give you feedback on the way you performed, you are assured of mastering that skill easily. When the day of presenting my icebreaker came, I was flawless, though deep inside I was afraid. Nonetheless, I spoke well and received awesome feedback from my evaluator, Sammy Kanjala. My new-found confidence propelled me to engage an extra gear in learning public speaking and leadership skills.

As the years went by, I was chosen to be Club President. That year, the members of the club chose to abscond meetings and I got frustrated to the point of considering quitting as the only option at hand. However, something inside me urged me to hang on and keep learning. "Never quit", was the message I heard within me, "as winners never quit and quitters never win". Meetings were conducted and only three to five members attended these meetings. What intrigued me during these meetings was the passion of the members who were readily available for them. I then urged myself that as long as I had these members, I was ready to keep learning and leading the team. Despite my courage and resilience, my term ended with the club performing poorly and having lost a lot of members.

Be Willing to Take Up Challenges

As my term came to an end, I felt relieved that a new team would take over from ours. My dream of relinquishing my duties was shattered as I was chosen to run a second term as Club President. I had no choice but to accept the responsibility. This time with the assistance of the club coach, Soustain Chigalu, we breathed new life into a club that was dying. We managed to recruit new members and had great meetings. My term ended on a good note and then a new team came in.

Apart from being Club President, I took up other leadership roles like Vice President Membership, responsible for recruiting new members. Our club's performance was great and so I was voted in as Vice President of Education, a Chief Operating Officer in other words. It was my duty to make sure that every member was working smartly towards achieving his/her educational goals. I also made sure that new members were assigned mentors to assist them through their communication and leadership skills development journey. I must say that I managed this role amazingly well.

While serving the club in various leadership roles, I chose to become a mentor to new members who needed guidance and direction in their public speaking and leadership skills learning. I took this challenge seriously in order to learn: learn from other people's experiences and aspirations. Learn from other people about their drive in setting their goals. Learning to listen attentively to other people. Yes, while I took these protégés through the process of goal setting, I became inspired by the outcome of the goal-setting sessions I had with them. People have definite and great goals in life that will allow them to leave this world a better place than they found it. These insights, which I acquired and absorbed during the mentoring sessions I had with my fellow Toastmasters, helped me a lot in improving myself.

All these experiences I have gone through and shared with you have helped me to find my why. I have come to realize that I was born a teacher, a great leader whose only purpose is to develop people. Helping people find themselves and live their lives in full is my grand task. Seeing people lead great lives after finding their purpose is the reason for my joy. Life is amazing and beautiful the moment we discover and live out our purpose.

By the way, have you ever wondered why you are still breathing today? Have you asked yourself why you are here? People are created to live life, life in its fullness. But we tend not to live life to the full as we tire ourselves with the fears and worries of things that cannot lead us to our great selves: our true purpose, in other words, our chief aim. The moment we become aligned with our purpose and see it as already achieved each day, we reinforce the message in our subconscious mind to propel us into working towards achieving it. Set time aside for the discovery of your why, your purpose. This, then, will be the compass that will lead you to live your life to the full. I urge you, reading this sentence now, to stop going further until you find out your why. Please take your time, it is imperative that you discover your why.

Stick to Your Goals in Order to Live Your Purpose

Your purpose will not be realized unless you set up goals that scare you yet are somewhat achievable. Goals can be daily, weekly, monthly, and annually. These goals should range from mental, physical, emotional, and spiritual. We all must learn to set up our personal goals and constantly evaluate ourselves to see whether we are on course or not.

Through regular self-evaluation, we then change the course of action wherever and whenever we discover that we have been derailed. It is by achieving our daily goals that we can in turn conquer our weekly goals. By achieving our weekly goals we then realize our monthly goals, which finally give us the ripple effect of achieving our yearly goals. Daily small conquests lead to weekly conquests that then lead to monthly conquests and finally yearly conquests. Such a goal-oriented life, a life focused on goal actualization, leads to us living life to the full. Just as an organization sets goals at the beginning of its financial year, to be guided by these towards its mission, I challenge you that to live a life of purpose, you need to equally set personal goals that, no matter what, you shall achieve in that particular year. These goals are the stepping stones to the accomplishment of your purpose in life. Hence, I now challenge you to find yourself a notepad and a pen to write down your goals with timelines against them.

It is said that a goal without a timeline is only a dream. To realize your dreams, or to make your dreams come true, learn to give your goals timelines; the specific time in which they will be achieved. Is it a month from the time of setting them? Or a year? Or three years? This is a vital exercise that will give you a competitive advantage over others who have never thought of goal setting as one of their priority areas in life. Also, remember that you are accountable for your actions towards achieving these goals. When you take full responsibility for achieving these goals, you work towards achieving them no matter how tough the ride might be. In the end, you will find yourself living the dream life you were meant to live. Be among the 5% of the population that is living life in full because they have realized the importance of goal setting.

Your time is now. If they did it, why can't you do it? If they made it in life, why can you not make it as well? You were meant for greatness and nothing less, so why are you living an average life? Turn your life around. Set up challenging goals for yourself today, then become one of the greatest sons and daughters of this world. This world needs leaders who can assist others to realize their dreams as well. It starts with you. Be a legend.

Strategize to Realize Your Goals

Goals are posts that stand along the way to our greatness. These posts are like the mirrors on our cars. Without these mirrors, chances are high that we can find ourselves involved in fatal accidents. To avoid accidents in life, we need these posts (goals) that can lead us to our destination (purpose). The more effectively we use these mirrors, the less likely we find ourselves involved in car accidents. We are taught how to use car mirrors for the good of our lives. Equally, in life, our goals can only be achieved if we become fully aware of how we can achieve them. I call this the 'how' – means to a cause. We need strategies that can help us realize our goals to live our lives to the full. It is not enough to set up goals in life and leave them like that and expect profound results. Taking action towards achieving these goals is mandatory. Without action expect no progress. Goals are achieved once strategies or means are put in place to achieve them. Having set up your goals, below each goal, you need to put down means of achieving each one of these goals.

For instance, if your goal is to travel to South Africa on any designated day, you need to know full well how you shall travel there. Is it going to be by bus? By plane? Or by ship? Similarly, when you have set up your personal goals, these goals need strategies to make them come true. What strategies do you have in mind to achieve the goals you have set up for yourself? List them down, assess them. Are they the best strategies to lead you home? Are they the most cost-effective strategies that will make you happy at the end of your journey? Think about and list them down, as many as they may be, and select the best three to four strategies that can make you the victor at the end of the competition. Be sure to take your time with this process because you are building a new personality within you: an achiever, someone unique and special, someone never led by the crowd, someone who never spends their entire life just imitating others. Yes, you can turn your life around. You can be the best version of yourself. John Mason tells us that we are all born originals and we should not die as copies. Find the original version of yourself and become the best of yourself. Your moment is now.

Inquisitiveness leads us to find our purpose in life. Not only should we find our why through inquisitiveness, but we should also be alert or aware of what other people say about us. We all need constructive feedback from others. Our personal experiences and the utterances of other people about us play a great role in us finding our purpose. We also need to take a step further to live our life in full: we need to work at constantly improving ourselves. We improve ourselves every time we are ready and willing to take up challenges. It is through facing challenges head-on that we come to know ourselves fully.

We are urged to set up stretch goals; goals that turn our heads this way and that way, as we sleep, to live a life of purpose. These goals are always supported by strategies - the means to realize them. Most of us have and still are, living a life without purpose because we never find the time to write down our goals and strategies that can lead us to our purpose in life.

In the next chapter, you shall come across the need for you to take a journey into continuous personal development. The moment you start to work on continuously improving yourself, that is the moment you embark on living your dream life. I urge you to turn to the next chapter and tap into the wisdom of continuous personal development.

Chapter Three

CONTINUOUS SELF-IMPROVEMENT: MAKE IT YOUR PRIORITY

"The road to success is always under construction."
– Lily Tomlin

In the previous chapter, we enjoyed the essence of having the child mind - a mind of wonder, a mind that is curious all the time. We also noted the importance of setting our priorities straight. Furthermore, we learned that paying attention to our experiences; learning from what people say about us; and learning to set goals, helps us awaken the giant within us. It's this giant in us, once awakened, that can lead us to live a purposeful life.

In this chapter, let us embark on a journey of continuous personal development. A journey of continuous learning, a learning that will equip us with the skills necessary to meet the demands of the 21st Century, and thereby live our life to the full.

Continuous Personal Development

How many of us remember the day we were taken to school for the first time? Does it ring a bell? What about you crying all day at school for your parents, or whoever had escorted you there, and left you alone in the hands of strangers? Or the teacher who soothed you and helped you to stop crying? Within a few days of attending classes, interacting with and making new friends, going to school turned into a MUST for both you and me. We fell in love with learning and began eagerly looking forward to the next day each time we were told it was time to knock off and called it a day. We had stories to tell our parents when we got back home. Stories ranging from learning the alphabet to counting numbers from 1 – 10. This newfound knowledge became the talk of the day during our childhood. We were ever curious to learn even more than the previous day. Why? Childhood is the moment of discovery. A moment of acquiring as much knowledge as we can like a sponge absorbs water.

But, as time elapses, and we move on in life, we lose those vibes. All the curiosity and interest in learning something new falters. It dries up just as flowers wither during dry and hot days. Living without curiosity leads us to live an average life. Sometimes the problem becomes our stagnation in our little successes; what John C Maxwell calls *destination syndrome*. This is the life most people regret living while on their deathbeds as they recall how they wasted their time pursuing useless stuff. I am convinced you are not one of them, living aimlessly and carelessly, or living a stagnant life. A stagnant life, like stagnant waters, stinks. Maxwell indicates that if you want to take the success journey, you must live a life of growth.

To progress in life, especially now when technology is threatening the livelihood of mankind, we must resuscitate or awaken the child in us to help us continue learning. We are faced with job cuts because robots are taking over our jobs, and in the process we are rendered redundant or useless. Declared redundant leaves us clueless, aimless, weak, and directionless. In this state, we can never live our dream life: a life of purpose. However, with the giant awakened, we turn into wise men and women who ask intelligent questions and look out for our gifts. Each one of us is gifted in one way or another, but due to our failure to attend to ourselves, we bury our gifts. We find ourselves in the din of noise, digital noise, which leads us to lose our sense of focus. While lost in the din of the digital noise, with willpower, we can reclaim our greatness.

Every human being is created for greatness. We can reclaim this greatness the moment we learn to love ourselves. Loving ourselves implies that we do all we can to put ourselves first in everything we do. I am not propagating selfishness here. What I mean is that charity begins at home and also that it is only after we have learned to love ourselves that we may be able to reach out to others in love. And one of the ways to show ourselves love is continuous learning. The moment you and I turn to continuous learning is the moment we get started with living our life to the full. The challenge you and I have is unlearning the behavior of laziness that leads us to settle for less. We are all called to stand for a cause in this world. This cause can be realized if you and I embark on learning some new and unique skills that can turn us into the most sought-after resources. New and unique skills differentiate us from the rest of the people around us. Remember that the education system all of us went through made us uniform - a commodity no different from the other. Having the same qualifications acquired from the various tertiary schools we went to, made us all the same. We can change the game only if we allow ourselves to learn new and unique skills.

In a nutshell, you need to upgrade yourself. What are you good at that no one else can beat you at? Only when you learn a new skill and do it repeatedly can you gain experience. To up the game, you must engage in the repeated practice of a new skill until it becomes you, you become the master, and eventually the leader in terms of that skill. You indeed have the greatness within you to learn, do, and become the master of anything you choose. So, what's stopping you?

It's Time to Determine Your Own Path

We cannot face our challenges with old skills, yet these are the skills most of us are stuck on acquiring. We are a people that have been blinded by technology and social media. Instead of taking advantage of its ability to help us more easily explore and understand issues holistically, we are busy wasting our time liking and commenting on our friends' posts on social media.

Great men and women living their lives in full today, are using the same technology to advance their existence; they are posting skills that we need to learn to survive in the 21st century. They are leading us by example, yet we are still blind to see their posts. We are not interested in searching for answers to our new challenges. We think we are doomed yet we forget that our forefathers had to change to survive the new challenges they came across. They saw the opportunity in the challenges they met. They did not view challenges as stumbling blocks but as set-ups for advancement and success. They adapted to the change in their environment by changing themselves and by learning or teaching themselves new skills. We don't want to spend time alone feeding our minds new knowledge that can deepen our skills - skills that are needed in the 21st century. We are a people who are not interested in finding new ways of improving our lives.

Technology has advanced to levels that at the click of a button, we can easily get as many answers as possible to any question we have. Why are we failing to improve ourselves with the same technology that we use to focus our attention on trivia and social media? The same energy we spend on following every post, every tweet, and every update on social media can be turned into an asset that can improve us by staying inquisitive and learning new skills.

Robert H, Schuller said, "*Tough times never last, but tough people do.*" The truth is that great people in this world - the legends; those who have left lasting impressions on other people's lives - worked really hard on improving themselves. These great men and women attained great heights by toiling upwards in the night while their friends were sleeping and snoring. They learned to challenge themselves. Like Martin Luther King Junior once said, "If you can't be the pine on top of the mountain, be the best shrub in the valley; if you can't run, walk; if you can't walk, crawl; but by all means keep moving." They, too, prepared themselves for the challenges they encountered by learning new skills meant to resolve those challenges. They spared time to teach themselves new skills. They made mistakes and yet, made them again. Through these mistakes, they learned and acquired new skills after consistently and relentlessly pursuing what they were keen to learn.

Hardships in life build men and women of substance, however, this is not the way most people perceive them nowadays. We are a people who see only darkness and doom at the end of the tunnel. Instead of dwelling on the darkness in the tunnel, why not challenge ourselves, through the acquisition of new skills, to see the light. Learning is a continuous process; a process that takes time to acquire these new skills and to get them to stick in us. Continuous personal development differentiates us. John C Maxwell says that successful and unsuccessful people vary in their desire to reach their potential. He says that, "Self-improvement is the way one needs to go if they want to reach their potential." Continuous personal development at our own pace creates champions in us. We need to relentlessly, over time, immerse ourselves in the act of acquiring a new skill.

The 21st century has brought with it new opportunities for growth and greatness. If our interest is in living our lives to the full, continuous personal development is the only remedy to greatness in this era. Leo Tolstoy says, "everyone thinks of changing the world but no one thinks of changing him/herself." It is the individuals who are creative and who easily adapt to change that will survive in the 21st Century. You can make yourself creative and adaptable to change by continuous learning. Embarking on a self-taught personal journey is the best way to reach great heights; heights only a rare breed of men and women have reached. My questions to you are:

What is your plan for personal growth? Which areas of your life need improvement?

How do you see yourself ten years from now?

Are you going to remain relevant?

Are your skills going to still be vital at that time?

....

....

....

....

Please take your time in answering these probing questions. It's your responsibility to make yourself a rare resource, so take that ownership seriously. The choice is yours: to either be a legend or an average individual. Make that choice now, and not later. You are absolutely meant to live the life of a legend, the life of a great man or woman. But to realize this dream, you have to take the necessary steps now to get you there. You, and no one else but you, are in total control of your life. Yes, you matter, which is all the more reason I am urging you to make that tough choice now to realize your dream in the future.

I chose to lead a great life. After choosing what I felt were my favorite skills to learn, I had to involve people whom I looked up to, to assist me in my pursuit for growth. You too can do the same. There are a lot of men and women out there willing and ready to take you through the journey to excellence.

Continuous learning through attending business conferences, seminars, and online courses differentiates us from those who do not spare time to upgrade themselves. Have you ever thought of improving yourself through attending any conferences, seminars, or online courses? If not, you better think twice and get started. There are a lot of affordable online courses that can bring out the best in you and differentiate you from the rest. One such site is Udemy (www.udemy.com). Not only can you raise the bar through conferences, seminars, and online courses, but there are also schools and clubs like Toastmasters International in your country that can take you to great heights attained by only a great few. Yes, standing out is the prerequisite for those who believe in becoming great leaders who matter in this world. YouTube (www.youtube.com) is another great medium with lots of profound courses that can empower you in the areas you deem fit for yourself. Act now, not later, for you were meant to be the best in the world.

Are You Reading?

When did you last read a book? Any book? I want to encourage you to turn yourself into an avid reader. The time you invest in reading books you have never read in your life will reward you tremendously. Every time you engage your brain in learning anything new, you stretch and grow your brain's neurons. By growing these neurons with new knowledge, you enhance the way you see or perceive the world and the people you meet in life. With the proliferation of smartphones, life has been simplified. Access to great books that can transform your understanding and decision making is at the click of a button. For once, turn off your attention from the digital noise and engage your brain in learning new skills.

Learning by interacting with only quality people (OQP) - parents, elders, friends, workmates, mentors, and coaches - brings about the greatness in us. Equally, burying ourselves in books we have never read will bring us to heights rarely attained by the 95% of the world population. Getting ourselves back to school, online or offline, can take us on a journey to realize our dream and live a fulfilled life.

These insights will be meaningless or empty if you do not take action now. You need not live an average life as though you never had an opportunity to learn these truths and read many other amazing and insightful books.

Bear in mind that you and I, using our five senses, do acquire and retain new knowledge through a process called **OLA**. This is as much the same as the timeless *See, Judge* and *Act* method of Social Analysis. Putting this system in action, allows us to become the game-changers. **OLA**, therefore, is an acronym for:

<table>
<tr><td>**O:**</td><td>Observe</td></tr>
<tr><td>**L:**</td><td>Learn</td></tr>
<tr><td>**A:**</td><td>Apply</td></tr>
</table>

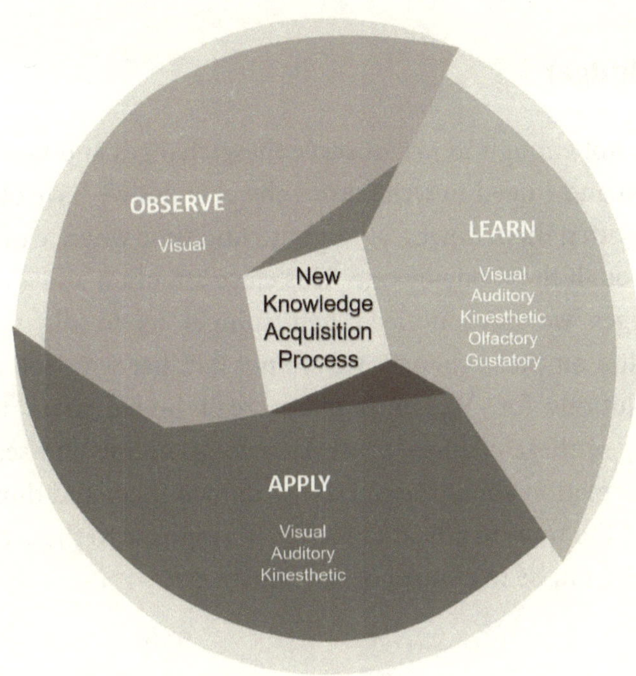

Figure 1 – New Knowledge Acquisition Process

As shown in Figure 1 above, OLA has been expounded below for your edification:

Observe (See)

With our eyes open and on the alert, you and I need to pay attention to the changes that are taking place in our places of work; the industry we are in; the political and economic climate; as well as the social and technological systems that are emerging. Observing these changes gives us an upper hand over those who are working and operating in their work and business in a usual and routine manner. I am, therefore, urging you to start now to learn to keenly observe all the changes that are taking place in the environment you are in, in order to be able to win in it.

Learn (Judge)

It is not enough to just observe these changes and take note of them. You and I need to write down the changes we have observed. Having written them down, we ought to find time where we can start going through them one by one. This close attention and analysis of the changes we have noticed will compel us to dig for more information on those changes we are not familiar with and have no ready solutions for. We must either read books so as to learn intimately of these changes or we have to go online and search for more information about them. Having known them and thoroughly learned of the ways to adjust ourselves in response to these changes, empowers us to be in control of our situations.

Apply (Act)

Winners, having observed and learned of the changes around them, put into action the strategies that will allow them to be on top of their game. Applying the new strategies to the observed changes gives us the power to be relevant and to survive in turbulent times such as now when new technologies keep coming. If you had been working and doing business in a *laissez-faire* manner, you better think twice before you find yourself booted out of work and business. This is not the time to sleep but to stay awake all the time, hustling and applying all the necessary strategies to meet the demands of the 21st Century.

Be always an observer (one who sees what is happening around them), and a learner (processing all that you observe), and remember that applying (a person of responsive action) or putting into action newly acquired knowledge makes you and I the game changers of our time. This is our time to hustle to win the game.

In summary, we have learned that getting onto the journey of self-improvement; learning from and listening to OQP (only quality people) and having an interest in online courses from sites like Udemy and YouTube; as well as joining clubs like Toastmasters International, can help us acquire new and unique skills. These new and unique skills can differentiate us from the rest. This differentiation can unleash the greatness in us.

In the next chapter, you are going to learn the importance of valuing time: a unique and rare resource. A resource we can never reclaim once lost. How are you using your time? Are you wasting it on trivia, or are you using it for your good?

Chapter Four

TIME: HOW VALUABLE IS IT TO YOU?

"Men do not let anyone seize their estates, and if there is the slightest dispute about their boundaries, they rush to stones and arms; but they allow others to encroach on their lives – why, they themselves even invite in those who will take over their lives. You will find no one willing to share out his money; but to how many does each of us divide up his life! People are frugal in guarding their personal property; but as soon as it comes to squandering time, they are most wasteful of the one thing in which it is right to be stingy."
– Seneca

In this world of today, people spend a lot of their time attending to the various demands of life, ranging from work obligations, family needs, business pressure and digital noise. All these are the pressures of life that are causing us stress. However, I believe that you will agree with me that, in modern times, there is one demand that has taken up much of our time: digital noise; be it Facebook, Instagram, Twitter, WhatsApp, Telegram *et al.* The list is endless. A day cannot pass by without both you and I attending to one or more of these.

Immediately when we wake up, we pick up the phone to check updates on Facebook, Instagram, Twitter, and messages on WhatsApp and many more such platforms. While driving to work, church, or any other social gathering, you find yourself glancing at your phone the moment a notification pops up.

We may be with friends at a party or any social gathering, yet find ourselves glued to our phones chatting and laughing with someone sharing messages with us on our phones; dividing our attention between the friends we are with physically and our phone messages or updates, if not, ignoring the friends we are with altogether. We are mostly engaged in multitasking: doing too many things at the same time to the extent that either all suffer or one of them suffers. Why? We cannot be servants of two masters.

When you get onto a bus, taxi, or a train, going to work or coming from work, what do you see? People who are glued to their phone screens, who have plugged earphones into their ears. People who have chosen to enjoy those precious moments with virtual friends at the expense of those sitting close to them, missing business opportunities, potential customers, and potential investors. You see people nodding or leaning in, actively showing interest, and laughing with their faces radiant; and you wonder why. Someone far has sent them a joke that they are reading on their phone screen. Some will even jump off their seats, why? Tickled by messages from a virtual friend. Slowly but surely, we are losing grip with our true selves. Our values are now upside down. Our intellectual capacity is slowly but surely getting lost in the process. Our attention to the most important and valuable things is slowly dying a natural death. What is becoming of us? Cyber zombies? Addicted to digital noise? Why us? Why now? Have you ever thought of this?

Imagine yourself waking up to a new world without technology. How would you react? That moment when you wake up and immediately pick up your phone to check updates on Facebook,

Instagram, Twitter, Flickr, and messages from the various groups you are part of on WhatsApp or Telegram, only to find yourself face to face with a blank screen. What would your reaction be? Awe, joy, wonder, anger, disappointment, or sadness? Would you curse the world? Would you find yourself time to absorb the abrupt and sudden change? You alone have the answers to all these questions. Think about it and see whether you are using your attention and time wisely.

As you do, take time to acknowledge that you are losing out by not sharing great moments with your loved ones or playing with the most valuable asset in your life. The asset no one can ever give you back once it is lost; that asset is time. No wonder an unknown author said, '*time is money*'. While everyone is fully engrossed in social media, one thing for sure is that we are losing time for ourselves. We are losing time to assess ourselves so as to unearth our gifts, strengths, and weaknesses, even discovering our purpose in life. Time to discover who we truly are. Time to find ourselves. Time to live that dream life.

Why have we chosen to live this empty life? Why have we all put our energies into something that is robbing us of our most valuable asset - time? How do we want to be remembered when we are gone? What legacy are we going to leave? When are we going to find ourselves alone without these gadgets, thinking about our purpose in life? How can we be of impact to this world when we do not even have time to ourselves? Why are we afraid of facing ourselves?

We are a people who can easily find fault in others while we cannot see our own shortfalls. We tend to be great advisors when it comes to helping others live fully, but we can't take the time to find fault in ourselves, in order to correct ourselves and live fully. We are very good at gossiping and wasting time; following and commenting on every post our friends put on social media, yet we cannot find time to see through own ourselves.

It is Not Too Late

It's never too late to find ourselves. It's never too late to live the life we have dreamt of. All we need now is a change in focus. It's now time we learn from others how to find ourselves. It's now time we learn where to place our attention and utilize our time wisely. It's time to reclaim our glory. We have lost nothing looking at the way we have lived, but we have learned a lot from the experiences of our life. It's now time to turn around, do a soul search and find out what is holding us back from our true selves. How satisfied would you be if you could learn to direct your life into fruitful engagements? Engagements that will see you fully contributing to the wellness of others.

It takes courage, will power and resilience to make that U-turn. It will be worthwhile, however, let's face it, we are all called to live life to the full. Each one of us is blessed with unique gifts meant to be fully utilized. Why are we choosing to live an average life? Why are we settling for less? Why, on earth, are we just surviving instead of striving? Yet we know that we are great. Yet we know we are here to live fully. This can be achieved if we spend time digging deep within in search of self. Become aware of yourself. Take time to face your fears; the fears of knowing yourself fully. It's better to conquer your fears and live happily after the victory than to live an average life full of regrets because you chose to run away from knowing yourself well.

Take the time now to decide that you will use your time wisely.

Time in Solitude

The great men and women we know of today took time to themselves. They had time to search within themselves to find the gifts they possessed. They had time to ask themselves important questions like who they were; what they were here for; what their strengths and weaknesses were; how they could use their strengths to contribute to the well-being of others in this world; and how they could improve and turn their weaknesses into fortes. This is how those men and women of valor found themselves. This is how they made it in life.

Why can't we tap into these people's wisdom? Why can't we read their autobiographies and pick up some gems from their experiences? You might say, "I don't have resources to gain access to these great men and women's autobiographies." And you might be right. But I would like to challenge you: the very same technology you are busy using for fun, for chatting on social media, you can use to gain access to these people's books online. Through these men and women's books, you can tap into their wisdom to assess yourself. I urge you, now is your time to find yourself. Now is your time to find those techniques these men and women used to discover themselves. By mirroring and modeling them, doing exactly what they did to find themselves, you too can find yourself. There could never be saints if there had been no people who spent time checking their actions, questioning them, correcting them, and improving upon them where necessary. Emulate them.

Take advantage of Google Search, TED Talks, YouTube and other online platforms to help you discover yourself. There are online tests available and awaiting you to access them. There are videos you can watch online that once watched, will leave you bewildered, breathless, astounded, and blaming yourself for taking too long to discover who you truly are. Press those buttons on your phone to access these online questionnaires and videos that can help you unleash the giant in you. You are the most valuable asset the world has ever had - why spoil your gifts? Make that decision now to know yourself well, and know that the answers are within your reach - through your smartphone. Explore the world with it; learn from using your smartphone well. Find that person you have been afraid of all this time by using your smartphone. Stop being an intimate stranger to yourself. You matter. You are one of the greatest works of art God has ever created.

What is the Importance of Time?

Brian Tracy, in his book titled, *Time Management,* states that time is the one indispensable and irreplaceable resource of accomplishment. It is your precious asset. It cannot be saved, nor can it be recovered once lost. He further alludes that everything you must do requires time, and the better you use your time, the more you will accomplish, and the greater your rewards will be.

To be effective and healthy, we need to manage our only irreplaceable asset – time - really well. You and I are a people who are hungry for meaning and purpose in life. Managing our time well can lead us to find the meaning and purpose of our lives. How do we find meaning and purpose in life? By setting time aside to be alone. During these lonely moments, we ask ourselves vital questions that assist us in finding our purpose.

We live in a world where everything is moving at a very fast pace. To be on top of our game, we need to be in total control of things happening around us. Be it at work, home, club, or any other place we find ourselves. We need to know how much time we have allotted to each activity to live a life of accomplishment.

Whenever you accomplish whatever you have planned to achieve, you find yourself living an accomplished and fulfilled life. Who does not want to live an accomplished and fulfilled life? No one. Can an accomplishment come to us on a silver platter? No. It requires us to sweat every day. Every time we achieve any goal, we find ourselves satisfied. Why? It is because we see ourselves as achievers. This takes place only when we plan our activities well and assign them time for completion. These activities must be in line with our purpose in life.

What Happens if I Do Not Take my Time Seriously?

All the people who have managed to live greatly, having achieved a lot in life, have had to guard their time jealously. They had to make sure that they allot time to the most important activities that were in line with their purpose. Without us guarding our time, assigning it to the most important activities, and assessing whether or not we are on course, we are bound to live an average life.

Without proper time management, we tend to lose control of ourselves. We find ourselves panicking, doing the most important things last minute and haphazardly. Or we find ourselves attending to other people's priorities at the expense of our own goals. This happens because we choose not to plan our activities and allocate time to them. In the end, we find ourselves frustrated and stressed, having failed to meet our obligations. It can be a regret for both you and I to die having achieved nothing worthwhile because we chose to dwell on things that did not matter the most in life.

How to Better Utilize Your Time

To begin with, for us to learn something new, whether it be a habit or behavior, it demands of us to change the way we used to do things and behave. We are expected to make a complete U-Turn. Change is not easy. It's demanding. "Change is hard at the beginning, messy in the middle and gorgeous at the end", states Robin Sharma. And to achieve success in doing something new requires a minimum of 21 days as stipulated by psychologists.

Like when we learned to read a book, or write, or drive a car, we had to put a lot of effort in the beginning to understand the new ideas well using our conscious mind. We had to put in a lot of effort, day and night, repeatedly, until these new ideas became second nature to us. It is in doing this that we come into our being (become masters of our game). Equally, to learn to use time well, we need to take baby steps every day until we come to a point where managing our time well becomes a part of us. To manage our time well, we need first to realize our shortfalls. We need to take steps that will lead us to learn how to use our time well. We have to repeatedly practice, every day, how to use our time well until we master time management to the extent that we are happy with the results we now realize. Then and only then, can we see the change we wanted.

There are several strategies that you can use to manage your time well. You can find and learn these strategies if you spare some time to read these two books by Brian Tracy, ***Eat the Frog! 21 Great Ways to Stop Procrastinating and Get More Done in Less Time*** and ***Time Management***. For those who cannot manage to get these books, here are the three strategies that I have come across and find very useful, and therefore recommend them to you:

1.   Plan Each Day in Advance

*"Planning is bringing the future into the present so
that you can do something about it now."*
– Alan Lakein

The moment you learn to plan and put on paper the major activities for your next day is the moment you start using your time effectively. You must spare some time in the evening before going to sleep to write all the activities you plan to work on tomorrow. As you go to sleep, these activities remain in your mind, and you can easily manage these activities well the next day since you subconsciously started thinking of the way you will tackle them. Hence, I urge you to start planning your day in advance and see how effectively you will be in accomplishing your planned assignments.

2.   Focus on Key Result Areas

*"When every physical and mental resource is
focused, one's power to solve a problem multiplies
tremendously."*
– Norman Vincent Peale

Brian Tracy states that as an individual working for any organization or for yourself, you need to ask yourself this question; 'Why am I on the payroll?' Unless you and I know why we are on the payroll in our organizations, we cannot perform at our best, get paid more, and get promoted faster than expected.

Brian Tracy continues to say, in the same book, that your job can be broken down into about five to seven key result areas, seldom more. These represent the results that you absolutely, positively must attain to fulfill your responsibilities and make your maximum contribution to your organization.

He then goes on to define a key result area as something for which you are completely responsible. It is an activity that is under your control. It is your responsibility to make sure that this activity is accomplished by all means. Your fate as an employee is determined by the accomplishment or failure to carry out this activity.

3.   Apply the Law of Three

"Do what you can, with what you have, where you are."
– Theodore Roosevelt

Brian Tracy states that the three core tasks that you perform contain most of the value that you contribute to your business or organization. He further says that your ability to accurately identify these three key tasks and then to focus on them is essential for you to perform at your best. This is one of the strategies I use to accomplish my tasks daily in our organization. I learned this from one of my mentors, Andy Harrington, who inculcated in me the concept of minoring in major things and not majoring in minor things as evidenced by what most people do. By minoring in major things, I have seen myself managing my time and life well.

*"Only those who will risk going too far can possibly
find out how far they can go."*
– TS Eliot

Through allotting time to yourself, not only will you find the online tests and videos to assist you in your journey of self-discovery, there are also books that you can find that will take you through this process. Press those buttons on your phone, they will lead you to get any book you want for self-discovery. Imagine knowing who you truly are; how satisfied will you be? Imagine living the life you had dreamt of because you found yourself; how great will you feel? I am challenging you NOW to take that bold step to discover yourself. You really, really, really matter. Turn your smartphone into an asset that will make you one of the greatest people to have ever lived. Spare some time to download and read those amazing and great books. Books that contain wisdom and life insights you never knew existed, but are very impactful in terms of your well-being.

One day, while using my morning time block productively, I came across and started reading a book titled, **Reprogram Your Subconscious – 10 Secrets to Manifest Powerful Abundance in Your Life** by Jamie Cole. I was fascinated by what she writes in chapter 1, **The Journey to Finding Your Purpose**: she outlines 14 steps that we can use to discover ourselves, but I shall share with you only three of these. For the rest, it is your assignment to either buy a hard copy of this book or get a soft copy online.

The first step is *conducting a self-assessment for self-discovery.* This step starts with this great quote: "*There is no greater journey than the one that you must take to discover all of the mysteries that lie within you*", by Michelle Sandlin. Self-knowledge starts with a self-assessment, and self-assessment involves looking deep within yourself. She explains that the first step to a definite self-assessment is to be HONEST about you. She requests you and I to take a good look in the mirror and take time to study the person you and I see looking back.

She further states that you need to describe the person you see in the mirror using up to a total of 25 adjectives. "*Consider using both positive and negative adjectives. This exercise is important because you are being honest with yourself. Dig deep. Allow for self-discovery.*" (Jamie Cole)

The next step is to consider your likes and dislikes. *This is important to allow yourself to identify the root of your likes and dislikes.*

Write down the activities you love doing.

Which books do you enjoy reading?

What kind of people do you surround yourself with?

What are the activities you enjoy during your free time?

....

....

....

....

....

....

The second step is *getting to know the real you*. Again, this step is followed by this beautiful quote: "*Anyone can appear beautiful from afar. The real test of character is how you are to those nearest to you. Good character means that the closer someone comes to you, the more beautiful you are*", by Yasmin Mogahed

She insists that discovering your real self can be scary sometimes. It demands an understanding of your personal aspirations, emotions, and even spiritual values. It also involves knowing how best to fulfill the requirements you want in life. If you come to an understanding of all these aspects of life, then you are on the right path to self-discovery.

She reinforces the observation that what we usually focus on in our life is making a living (chasing money) and we tend to forget the spiritual part of our lives. We neglect the fact that we need to strike a balance between our physical, emotional, and spiritual being.

She emphasizes the need to look inside your soul and search for what it needs. It is important to note that we are not just a vessel but rather we have an inner self comprising of the soul which also yearns for satisfaction.

She further says that we need to be connected with ourselves and draw attention or move away from distractions outside. In most cases, our focus is turned towards meeting our external desires. There will never be a sense of fulfillment if we keep looking at the outside. In most instances, we are busy with the desire to meet the needs of the physical and this causes one to lose him or herself. Take time to meditate. It will help you realize and know yourself better.

Finally, she expresses that another way to help you discover your real self is by improving your relationship with others. It helps you to place your focus less on material gains and more on intangible values like love and honesty. We will feel more content when we improve our connection with others by making the people around us happy and by helping out where we can. This gives us more of a spiritual satisfaction.

The third and final step I want to share with you is, *"the value of spiritual self-discovery" (Jamie Cole)*. In the same vein, this step is followed by the quote: *"To make the right choices in life, you have to get in touch with your soul. To do this, you need to experience solitude, which most people are afraid of, because in the silence you hear the truth and know the solutions"*, by Deepak Chopra.

Jamie Cole impresses me when she states that when people embark on a journey of self-discovery, they tend to focus on the physical and emotional side of their personality. She also expresses that people rarely take into account the importance of spiritual self-discovery. We must take some time to explore the spiritual aspect of ourselves, she insists. As a result, we will discover a unique and different aspect of our personality we may not even have realized existed.

She stipulates that we are made up of physical, spiritual, intellectual, and emotional dimensions. We experience the universe through the individual and collective lenses of these dimensions.

On another note, in the process of using my time sparingly and jealously, I managed to download and tap into the wisdom of understanding the importance of self-knowledge in an insightful book titled - ***Out of Your Comfort Zone, Breaking Boundaries for a Life Beyond Limits*** by Emma Mardlin, Ph.D. In this book, you can gain access to great insights like going through *the zone test – which helps you determine your comfort zone level right now.* The essence of the zone test is *"to establish your current comfort zone and to highlight the aspects of your life that might be holding you back; right from the obvious things to the things you may not be consciously aware of. Using this introspective quiz, you will be able to see which zone you fall into and look at the areas in your life you can positively think differently about and change in order to push yourself forward to reach zone zero. This is the point at which you no longer have boundaries or irrational fears – just challenges that you know you'll quite easily smash as and when you need to, leaving you to enjoy a fulfilled and exhilarating life."*

In this same book, Emma takes you through the *"30-Day Resilience- Builder Challenges"*. Through this 30-day challenge, you will be engaged in activities that you had never thought of doing for the sake of *"reconditioning and transitioning your mind and body for positive change" (Emma Mardlin).* You will be challenged to participate in tasks you never imagined possible for you, to realize your great potential. We human beings are created great and unique, but we are deceived by the negativity that comes from our thoughts. Ever heard of the statement – "we become what we mostly think about"? Every time we bury ourselves in negative thinking, we subconsciously propel ourselves to become those thoughts. To realize our greatness, we must be fired up with positive energy emanating from positive thoughts, emotions, a healthy body, and spiritual grounding. "*Yes, you can*", as expressed by the former President of the USA, Barack Obama. I believe all of us have whatever it takes for us to live life to the fullest but we need to be cognizant of what will help us get there.

The final book that can also assist you in discovering yourself is titled ***The Gift in You: Discovering New Life Through Gifts Hidden in Your Mind*** by Dr. Caroline Leaf. In this book, Dr. Leaf offers a different perspective on self-discovery. She explains that each of us is gifted from birth. She begins chapter 1, **Uncovering Your Hidden Gift**, with a quote from the Bible: "*I knew you before I formed you in your mother's womb*" (Jeremiah 1:5 NLT). God, the Ultimate Being, gave each of us gifts we rarely recognize we have. We have sat on these gifts unknowingly without unleashing them to assist us in realizing our dreams. We have chosen to live miserably yet we are gifted with unique talents that can make us a force to be reckoned with. This implies that we are born with natural gifts that need us to unleash them.

In chapter 2 of her book, ***You are Not Your Score***, Dr. Leaf goes on to state that "*often, when we are grouped into boxes – learning disabled, gifted, right brained, left brained, overachiever, underachiever or any other box which seems to fit nicely at that time – that definition becomes a part of us. However, you are so much more than what any label can define you as.*"

She further makes a statement that: "*Thankfully, we are living in a revolutionary time. Using the latest research, we can now clearly prove that intelligence is not fixed but rather grows and develops with us as we use it. Just like your gift. You've had it inside of you all along, but it only grows and develops if you uncover it and use it properly."*

In chapter 7, **The Seven Pillars of Your Gift,** she says that *"there are seven pillars of your gift and each of the seven pillars of thinking is responsible for primary functions and particular characteristics."* She insists, *'This is the gifting principle: We do not all have the same gift'.* To keep your curiosity high, here is an outline of the seven pillars of your gifts:

- Intrapersonal Intelligence
- Interpersonal Thinking
- Linguistic Thinking
- Logical/Mathematical Thinking
- Kinesthetic Thinking
- Musical Thinking
- Visual/Spatial Thinking

By going through all seven pillars, you will be in a position to learn and know your natural gift. Having had the opportunity to understand yourself through your gift identification, you will then utilize this gift to live your life to the full. Yes, you are unique and very special; never look down on yourself. You are here to reveal and share the fruits of your gift to others, to improve others' lives, but only after you have unlocked these gifts. You and I are meant for greatness and nothing else, however, our thoughts tend to pull us the other way. St. Paul writes in Ephesians 2:10 that "we are God's handiwork, created in Christ Jesus to do good works, which God prepared in advance for us to do." I urge you to grab this book as well to learn and grow in realizing the gift you have inside. What we lack is an understanding of our gifts.

Can you see how empowered I must have felt having read those three books? This happened because I learned to use my time well. Just think about it, from the insights gathered from these three books mentioned in this chapter, you and I can now reinvent our lives. We are the captains of our ships and the courses of our journeys are our responsibility. You are now empowered to spend time alone; do a self-assessment; meditate; conduct a zone test; take up the 30-day challenge; and find your gift to live a great life. You are solely responsible for whatever life you live. The onus is on you so act now and see what lays in store for you.

Despite the challenges I come across in life, I now know I am in control. I am never shaken up by life's challenges because I have realized that I am above the circumstances I find myself in. Always I choose to remain calm and resolve these challenges with ease. Life's adversities and challenges come to everyone, but how we deal with them makes a real difference. In fact, it is said that the same sun that bakes clay melts butter! The sun is the same but the makeup of clay and butter differ. What are you made of? Be in charge of your circumstances. One circumstance can make one person better and another, bitter. The choice is yours! Live the dream life you have always wished you could. I have managed to live life with resolve because I spend most of my time alone, but not lonely. Every time I am alone I live in solitude and not in loneliness! Have you heard people shamelessly saying I am alone and lonely? A person who has discovered themselves and their gifts and purpose in life cannot suffer from loneliness just because they are alone. They will always find something to do to improve themselves or to add value to others. During my time of solitude, I am either reading a book I never came across while in college or school; meditating upon my life; or I am watching or listening to a video that teaches me a new way of living.

All these in the comfort of my home or while taking a walk in the jungle.

If you have been one of the people who have spent their time managing the demands and challenges of life without thinking of yourself first, you are now aware of how you can find yourself. Turn that smartphone into your goldmine: gold in the form of profound knowledge that will take you where you are meant to be.

Guard your time and guard it jealously. It is the only resource you cannot claim back once it is lost. Expend it on yourself; opening up to yourself fully. Take time to face that person you fear the most, yourself, with boldness - know him/her fully. Do not be content with remaining an intimate stranger to yourself; be the best friend and the closest person there ever is to you. You are the best there is, and ever will. It's a matter of willpower; the power to conquer yourself. If others have done it, have conquered themselves and are living happily, why can't you? Never settle for less when you were created for greatness. This happens in the stillness of solitude. In a place where you, alone, interact with yourself. This place can be at home - in your room where no one can interrupt you but yourself. Or you can choose to take a walk in the forest to cherish the beauty of nature. As you treasure the beauty of green or dried up brown leaves, and the sweet smell of a variety of beautiful flowers, you encounter yourself. Remember that "fortune favors the bold" - *a sorte favorece os audazes* in Portuguese. You either live your dream life or die average. The choice is no-one's but yours.

In summary, remember that the resource called time is indispensable and irreplaceable. Once gone, it can never be recovered. Use it wisely to find yourself through moments set aside for yourself alone: read books and watch videos on YouTube and TED Talks that will develop your skills to become the most sought after resource; exercise to live a healthy and happy life; and remember no-one but you is solely responsible for the outcome of the life you intend to live. Use your time wisely. Invest in your time profitably.

In the next chapter, you shall come across the need to recognize your self-worth. To appreciate yourself regardless of whatever circumstances you find yourself in. In most cases we as people look for approval from others in order to appreciate ourselves. That kind of behavior has its limitations that affect our way of doing things. It is important, therefore, that you and I learn to appreciate ourselves whether or not other people recognize our contributions. Go onto the next page and empower yourself through learning the importance of seeking self-approval in all you do in life instead of waiting for others to appreciate you each time you achieve something.

Chapter Five

SELF-WORTH, VALUES AND GOAL SETTING = PURPOSE

"The Sun, however, is unimpaired even in the midst of obstacles, and, though an object may intervene and cut off our view thereof, the Sun sticks to his work and goes on his course. Whenever he shines forth from amid the clouds, he is no smaller, nor less punctual either, than when he is free from clouds; since it makes a great deal of difference whether there is merely something in the way of his light or something which interferes with his shining."
– Seneca

Recognition Begins with You

Our life is influenced by both external and internal forces. With both forces pressing upon us, we tend to grow up being influenced either by the power from within us or by external forces like peer pressure. People who are influenced by the power within themselves live their life inside out; life in full and achieving their dreams. Why? They are in control of whatever influence that comes along their way. They do not seek approval from anyone but themselves.

Some people get sick if they don't receive approval from others. This is symptomatic of the fact that they do not sufficiently know and appreciate themselves. These people are influenced by external forces and tend to live life outside in. In other words, such people spend their entire lives trying to impress others instead of expressing the beauty of their inner person. Their decisions and actions are influenced by their colleagues at work, parents, and other people they interact with. They tend to believe whatever they are told by others to be true. In the end, they are always on the lookout for compliments or approval from other people to believe in themselves. Approval from others has become a drug to which they are addicted to.

While life is getting tougher by the day, and there are innumerable external forces like peer pressure, parents, work, digital noise, and many such influences exerting pressure on us, we tend to lose our sense of control. Instead of being in total control of our life, these external forces take over and control us. In the process, our focus on vital issues that matter most in life is lost. Distractions, wave after wave, are disturbing us to the extent that we cannot pay attention to important issues. Instead of pursuing our vision, goals, and plans, in order to soar high like an eagle, we are persuaded to pay attention to superfluous issues.

Approval from Others

Most people die for approval from others. When they are assigned a project at work, they willingly take up the responsibility of leading the team to execute that assignment. This they do while secretly holding on to the hope that they will receive applause for their achievements. In fact, they complete such assignments amazingly well. However, if they do not get acknowledged for discharging their duty well, they look at themselves as unworthy. To them, being recognized for great work done comes first.

Whenever we compulsively seek approval or recognition from others, we show that we are not mature enough. While feedback and recognition from others are important, mature people seek recognition from within themselves. Just imagine, does it matter whether we get noticed or not? Will you die if you don't get noticed for the completion of a project in the best manner possible? Self-worth is all we need to live life fully. The moment we learn to look at ourselves as special, talented, and unique, is the moment we shall not necessarily seek recognition or praise from others. Finding satisfaction in the successful completion of a project should matter more to us than praise from others. Don't live to impress the world but to express the beauty of who you are.

Jim Jones

There once was a young man whose name was Jim Jones. As a child, he worked hard at school and excelled in every subject he took. Every time he did well, he found himself very happy when either his teachers or parents congratulated him for the great grades. Because of these remarks, he kept on working hard. He always looked forward to words of encouragement from his parents and teachers whenever he did well.

He earned himself a place at the most prestigious university after passing his final examinations with flying colors. His parents were overjoyed that their son was doing very well at school and didn't stop patting him on the back for such an achievement. He felt great in his heart and this encouraged him to engage an extra gear when he got to the university. The young man excelled in his education. This he was able to do because he got used to the compliments he got every time he passed well. He got out of the university with a *cum laude* degree - an amazing accolade.

Jim Jones then found himself an extremely good job at a very popular company. He was over the moon for having secured this job. He discharged his duties well and indeed, his boss recognized him for his skills. In no time, Jim rose quickly through the ranks and file until he became the departmental head. He never settled for less. His drive was to reach the top of the hierarchy in this company. While performing his duties, he made it a point to execute them extremely well. His great skills were noticed by his bosses and yes, he was rewarded accordingly. Remember that Jim had grown up doing well because of the recognition other people showered on him. He became conditioned to the idea that being recognized was the only way to achieve something great in life.

One day, Jim received a white envelope while in his opulent and spacious office. He opened the envelope and pulled out a letter from it. He then began to read it and a few moments later you could see him jumping out of his chair in jubilance!

The message in the letter stated that he had been promoted to the role of Chief Executive Officer. He would be in charge of this company - his dream had come true. He was extremely happy with his feat and he went home with a big smile ready to share the wonderful news with his parents. It became a great moment for the family. Dancing, whistling, and ululations followed his good news. As usual, his parents congratulated him for this attainment and he was the man of the moment.

He went back to work and as expected, he performed extremely well. After some time, the company grew, and its bottom line improved tremendously. Due to his leadership, most of the workers there got noticed and were promoted. In his mind, since Jim was accustomed to receiving recognition, he expected to receive one yet again for the promotions of his workers. However, the recognition never came: it was his turn to notice other people's performance and reward them accordingly. He became unhappy that the tables - as far as he was concerned - had turned. He was looking for recognition but got none and frustration set in, and his performance started to decline.

Eventually, he thought of seeking assistance from a specialist in psychology; a life coach who could help him get his star performance back. He narrated his story of not getting any recognition for his amazing work as the Chief Executive Officer of this company. The life coach listened to him attentively and asked Jim to shed more light on his upbringing. Jim narrated everything from his accomplishments at school, university, and then at work. He told the life coach that his life was centered on the recognition he received every time he did well. That recognition is what propelled him to do amazingly well. He said that he also expected to get noticed as the CEO who was making the company produce great results.

The life coach looked him in the eyes and told him that he had reached the peak of the company hierarchy. As such, it was his turn to recognize others for their accomplishments. Jim insisted that he too needed recognition for his attainments but the life coach calmly told him that he ought to change this mindset. As a leader, he had reached the point where he needed to recognize himself. He had reached the level where his achievements needed no recognition from others but himself. The life coach took him through some self-worth coaching sessions. Through such training sessions, Jim learned to be happy with himself. He learned to accept himself as an achiever, a great leader and someone special with wonderful talents to change the world. In the words of Steve R Covey, he had to move from independence to inter-dependence and from effectiveness to greatness. While in the words of John C Maxwell, he had to multiply his greatness by investing in coaching and mentoring others. In the psychology of Abraham Maslow, Jim Jones had to move from self-actualization to transcendence. He continued producing great results and made other great contributions in his life.

Jim had the chance to meet a life coach who assisted him with appreciating himself first. He was taught how to value himself and lived a happy man afterward. Will you find yourself a coach to take you through the process of valuing yourself? If not, worry not. There are several options at your disposal. Make use of YouTube. There are several videos on the subject of self-worth. Watch and learn from them. If you believe in having someone take you through the process, you can get in touch with me to take you through this process. There is also another way of pursuing self-improvement in any area of your life which is identifying people who have done well in their life in the same area and making them your inspiration or role models. In his book called the *15 Invaluable Laws of Growth,* John C Maxwell tells us that "it is hard to improve when you have no one but yourself to follow." Remember that Les Brown once said, "*Someone's opinion of you does not have to become your reality*". You are someone special, you matter. Never get bogged down by people's opinions. In fact, if you become a slave of people's opinions, you will lead a miserable life. There are as many people's opinions about us as there are people and, remember, people's opinions of us can change anytime without our control. Failing to sleep because of what people say about you is not only careless but self-sabotage as well. No. Just appreciate them. Live life from inside out. Be in charge of your own life. If it is true that 'charity begins at home,' if truly we have to do unto to others what we would like them to do unto us and, if we have to 'love others as we love ourselves,' then real success can only flow through self-discovery, self-embrace, self-respect, and self-approval. To be in charge of your life, look at what you value most. There are several values that people who live life inside out pursue. You may be wondering what values are. Values are a guide that helps us make decisions as to what is right, good, valid, or meaningful. If an individual has difficulty clarifying his values, this can produce stress and feelings of anxiety, confusion, and helplessness.

The Importance of Values

If you establish values for yourself as an individual, you find that you better understand yourself and your feelings which gives you clarity in terms of relating to your future direction.

Our values should (ideally) determine our priorities in life. Life will then go generally well, and we will feel content and satisfied when the decisions we make match our values and priorities. However, when our decisions don't align with our values, that's when we start feeling like something is 'wrong' and this can lead to dissatisfaction, frustration, and in some instances, even bitterness or resentment. To avoid this, we must make a real effort to identify what our values are.

Without values, we look at the opinions of others as our reality. Hence to remain ourselves, grounded, focused, and centered, we must identify our values. It is said that those who do not stand their ground are easily blown by every wind like a yoyo. I urge you to have a thorough look at the list of values below and choose from them the ones that best represent you. This way, you will live to appreciate yourself and be a happy person.

Core Values

- Accountability
- Accuracy
- Achievement
- Adventurousness
- Authenticity
- Ambition
- Assertiveness
- Balance
- Belonging
- Boldness
- Calmness
- Carefulness
- Challenge
- Clear-Mindedness
- Commitment
- Community
- Compassion
- Connection
- Consistency
- Contentment
- Contribution
- Certainty
- Creativity
- Decisiveness
- Dependability
- Determination
- Devoutness
- Diligence
- Discipline
- Discretion
- Diversity
- Effectiveness
- Efficiency
- Empathy
- Enthusiasm
- Equality
- Excellence
- Excitement
- Exploration
- Expressiveness
- Fairness
- Faith
- Freedom
- Generosity
- Goodness
- Giving
- Growth
- Hard Work
- Honesty
- Hope
- Humility
- Ingenuity
- Identity
- Increase
- Justice
- Leadership
- Legacy
- Love
- Loyalty
- Obedience
- Openness
- Practicality
- Purpose
- Professionalism
- Progress
- Reliability
- Resourcefulness
- Restraint
- Relationships
- Security
- Self-Actualization
- Self-Improvement
- Self-Control
- Significance
- Selflessness
- Self-Worth
- Spontaneity
- Stability
- Sharing
- Teamwork
- Temperance
- Truth
- Thoroughness
- Timeliness
- Tolerance
- Traditionalism
- Trustworthiness
- Truth-Seeking
- Understanding
- Uniqueness
- Unity
- Vision
- Vitality

Take some time to go through these core values and think deeply about them. Then make a selection of the ones that resonate with you the most. You can choose a minimum of 10 values for yourself. Write these values in your diary so that you can read them frequently. That way you shall live a life of consistent self-appreciation. Then the opinions of others will not hurt you. Why? Because you will have come to know what drives your life.

The Importance of Values in Goal Setting

These values can also assist you in setting goals for yourself. Just as we set up goals for the company we work for, so too should we set up our personal goals. We spend some time once every year to come up with goals for various departments in our company. These goals are derived from the overall company goals for each financial year. We do this to assess whether we are on or off course as an organization. Changes are initiated when we realize that we have derailed, which helps us to get back on course.

Similarly, you and I must set up our personal goals at the beginning of every year. These goals should range from short, medium, and long term. They can range from daily, weekly, monthly, bi-annual, yearly, three year, and five year or more. By constantly reviewing our progress, we find ourselves on course and making great strides in life. Challenge yourself now and set up those stretch goals for yourself. You matter and you were meant to live life on your terms. Those people who lead great lives have goals and their life is led by these goals. With our goals written down and reviewed time and again, we shall surely lead a phenomenal life. A life in which we are in control of whatever is happening around us. A life where the opinions of others and the noise out there won't interfere with our livelihood. We shall remain focused and achieve a lot in our lives.

Yes, take that first step today to write down your goals, but only after you have written down your values which will form the foundation of everything you seek.

In summary, people who value themselves, who approve of themselves, achieve greatness in life. These are the people who live life inside out. They make their decisions based on what is important to them, while people who are always looking for approval from others are only happy with what other people tell them. Their decisions are influenced by the comments made by other people. These people live life outside in. Without any compliments from others, these people feel like life is hard on them. Which type of person are you?

Remember to also have personal values because, with them, you are assured of having a sense of direction since these have an impact on your goals. If you have no personal values, take time to come up with yours. Personal values help you to more easily set your goals.

In the next chapter, you shall come across an understanding of how we form the behaviors we have from the beliefs we have acquired from our parents, peers, elders, and society at large; and their impact on our attitudes, emotions, and thoughts. You shall also learn that as much as we did learn these limiting beliefs from our nurturers and society, we can unlearn them to free ourselves from mental slavery and live the life we desire to live. Turn to the next page and empower yourself through changing your beliefs which will have a ripple effect on your thoughts, emotions, attitudes, behaviors, and habits. The way you relate with others is dependent on what you think every day. These thoughts affect the way you react to what others say to you (your emotions); these emotions will then have an impact on the way you relate and see others (your attitudes); and these attitudes will influence the way you behave when in the company of others. Your behaviors will finally turn into habits, as we are what we repeatedly do.

HOW THOUGHTS BECOME HABITS

*"A man is literally what he thinks, his character
being the complete sum of all his thoughts."*
– James Allen

From the day you and I came into this world, we started experiencing a new wave of life. While we came into it with gargantuan and unimaginable dreams, believing in them and ourselves, forces outside of us started exerting pressure on us. As time went by, we started to learn what our parents, relatives, elders, teachers, culture, and society inculcated in us as the best practice. You and I were born original. We were very creative, growing up with a sense of pride and a total belief in these gargantuan dreams and ourselves. We looked at ourselves as people who could do and achieve anything in life. We were curious and inquisitive. We saw everything in technicolor. We had great dreams. Why? We were influenced by the power within us. In his book titled, **"*Thumbs Up! Five Steps to Create the Life of Your Dreams*"**, Joey Reiman states, "Yes, I believe we are all born geniuses, with the ability to dance, draw and sing. Then, school makes young adults out of us by taking the children out of us."

Over time, the people we encountered and got in touch with, and the experiences we shared with them started making us believe otherwise. The way we related with our family members at home, friends at clubs and others at social gatherings such as church and even work, started to have an impact on the way we looked at life in its totality. The sum total of these encounters and experiences gained, form our beliefs. During these interactions, we learned new ideas that either strengthened or even changed our beliefs. Some of these beliefs were passed on to us by our parents while young; others we learned from friends as we were playing with them or as we rubbed shoulders with them at school; and yet others we learned from the elders we related with. As we progressed in life, we engaged with people at church, social gatherings like wedding celebrations, funerals, and even parties.

During these encounters, we had time to pick up one or two thoughts that later on had an effect on our emotions; making us feel different than we had before. These feelings in turn influenced our attitudes towards certain things, eventually leading us to form beliefs that molded us to be who we are today. These beliefs over time led us to behave in a certain way; this behavior influenced our actions; and finally, you see that *as a man thinketh, so he becomes*, as stated by James Allen. In the end, we have taken on these beliefs as ours either actively or passively, through observation, chatting with or listening to elders and friends. One thing, though, is that we did not know that we were subconsciously becoming what we had learned from these interactions. We are what we are now because of the sum total of all the interactions we have had with all the people we have ever met - at school, church, work, clubs, while traveling or during meetings. In short, our values and belief systems and how we approach life are the products of socialization. In sociology, socialization is the process of internalizing the norms and ideologies of society. Socialization encompasses both learning and teaching and is thus, defined as "the means by which social and cultural continuity are attained", according to the book titled *Sociology,* **15th Edition (2013)** by John J Macionis.

Beliefs

A belief is defined, according to the **Roget's 21st Century Thesaurus in Dictionary Form**, as admission, conviction, judgment, mindset, presupposition, and understanding. Of particular importance is the definition of belief as a mindset. Mindset is a much talked about word. In our discussions with other people, we sometimes hear someone mention a certain individual as having either a positive or negative mindset based on the way this individual relates to others.

However, these beliefs are not a true representation of our true selves. We have learned the beliefs we possess, and we can also unlearn them. We have the choice to live with negative or positive beliefs. We are also responsible for continuing to live with the beliefs we acquired as children or to let them go. This power of choice is what truly resides in us: beliefs can be uprooted from within us by ourselves anytime we deem fit that they are no longer serving us.

You see, there are empowering and disempowering beliefs, positive or negative beliefs; and to excel in whatever we do, we must choose to live with empowering and positive beliefs. The disempowering beliefs serve us negatively since we end up being people who look down upon ourselves. The result is we live an average life and yet we are created to achieve greatness. Hence, we must always question our beliefs - whether they are serving us or not. Taking them wholeheartedly as the gospel truth, without questioning them, can lead to us losing ourselves. We were born great and very creative individuals, full of big dreams. We were born to rule the world with our unique gifts, but all these gifts are lost along the way as we move from our childhood to adult life. Whatever we had come with originally, the genius in us, the dreamer, the giant, and the hero in us, is lost with all the things we learn along the way to adulthood. Something worth mentioning is that most people become so afraid that they fail to live out their original selves: this fear prevents them from becoming what their creator intended for them. The great leader in the field of leadership, Myles Munroe, told us that the greatest riches are not in the platinum mines of South Africa or the goldfields of Ashanti-Ghana, but in the graveyards of men and women who never became what they were meant to become because of fear.

We learn of a lot of 'dos and don'ts' during our formative life journey, and these 'dos and don'ts have either a positive or negative impact on our progression in life. With all the information overload, we lose our true identity and we become what society dictates to us that we are. This is how we live for the rest of our lives - never questioning the labels assigned to us by our society. A society that acts and lives in a way contrary to who we truly are. We never question our society and blindly live according to its norms. Over time we blend with society, lose our greatness, settle for less, and become the average person that our society wanted to see. We live a normal life and anything we see happening in our society becomes normal. The genius in us, the child in us, inquisitive with lots of questions and yearning for answers, the daredevil, the risk-taker, the adventurer, dies a natural death. This child who was meant to live in us and lead us to achieve greatness in life, leaves us average, frustrated, having succumbed to society's way of living, and not our own. In the end, we become sleepwalkers. Don't forget John Mason's timeless advice, "You were born an original, don't die a copy". Have the courage to change the dark glasses through which you see reality. Question the origin of those glasses and if they are good for nothing, get new ones that will help you see reality in the most realistic way.

The Dangers of Sleepwalking

While sleepwalking, we do everything taking instructions from the subconscious. The subconscious listens to the body which then controls our mind. This makes us comfortable doing routine work, day in day out, without questioning ourselves as to why we are accustomed to such a life.

Conformity to group thinking erodes our independence. Anything society does is deemed right and worth pursuing. Any questions that come along in our lives are suppressed. Having lost our originality and creativity, we end up sailing against the wind, and consequently, we lead average lives.

That is why we have 95% of the total population living an average life or below the poverty line. Is this the life you want to live? A life of frustration and stress because you chose to conform to the society you live in? Why die alive while deep inside you is a power that can move mountains? A power that can unleash your potential.

Find yourself time to sit down alone and do a soul search to discover the type of beliefs that lead you every day. Remember, whatever you have learned can be unlearned. Choose to live with empowering beliefs to be the best in whatever you find yourself doing.

The Power of Beliefs

"Our programming, our conditioning from the day we were born, has created, reinforced, and nearly permanently cemented most of what we believe about ourselves and what we believe about most of what goes on around us," states Shad Helmstetter in his book titled, ***What to Say When You Talk to Your Self***. As we grow up, we learn a lot of things from the people we spend most of our time with and from the experiences we have had with them. Whatever they teach and share with us becomes part of us and this forms our beliefs.

Our beliefs, the things we consider and live by as truth or as correct, tap into how we have been programmed over time, and determine the way we behave during our encounters with others. These behaviors can assist us with either winning friends or losing them. Imagine yourself being open-minded whenever in the company of friends and others, engaging them in very productive discussions and never having unnecessary arguments in the process. How many friends would you attract?

On the flip side, see yourself having a closed mindset. Guess what then happens with you when interacting with friends, even your seniors at work: you find yourself justifying anything you have done. Even if you know that there is no point in backing the matter at hand or that you are in the wrong; while justifying your point, you end up hurting a lot of people along the way. Consequentially, you lose friends. The more reason you and I need to be aware of our behavior. Does it help us win friends or lose them? If it is negative and could lead to us losing friends, we need to adjust ourselves in order to win back those we have lost. Remember, we can either develop into greatness or die in poverty depending on the way we relate with other people.

The Ripple Effect of Our Thoughts on Our Behavior and Our Life

Our behavior affects our habits. With good habits, we attract friends, potential customers, and investors, even financiers of our businesses while, on the other hand, bad habits scare people away from us, and in the end, we find ourselves alone. Why? We become hot-tempered people, and no one will want to be close to us. Good habits, such as displaying warmth towards people we know or strangers, bring to us good tidings and fortune. To show you the importance of great behaviors that win friends and the ills of the worst behaviors that scare away friends, James Allen wrote in his book, **As A Man Thinketh**, "achievement, of whatever kind, is the crown of effort, the diadem of thought. By the aid of self-control, resolution, purity, righteousness, and well-directed thought a man ascends; by the aid of animality, indolence, impurity, corruption, and confusion of thought a man descends." He further stated that "a man may rise to high success in the world, and even to lofty altitudes in the spiritual realm, and again descend into weakness and wretchedness by allowing arrogant, selfish, and corrupt thoughts to take possession of him."

He finally said that "victories attained by right thoughts can only be maintained by watchfulness. Many give way when success is assured, and rapidly fall back into failure."

You can see that the root of our habits is thought. Watching over our thoughts gives us great feelings (emotions), and these great feelings allow us to become people of a positive attitude, believing in ourselves and then doing whatever work we get with a great attitude. These attitudes influence the way we work and relate with others (behaviors) and the result is us possessing awesome habits that win friends and grow our businesses or our professional careers.

On the other hand, our thoughts can lead us to develop bad feelings (emotions) that result in us having a bad attitude towards work and people. These bad attitudes negatively influence our behaviors, and what happens next? We turn out to be people with bad habits, the result being a loss of friends and no business at all. John C Maxwell points out that an attitude is a make or break ingredient of our lives and that great leadership rises on good relationships just as it falls on bad ones.

We are, therefore, challenged to be alert or vigilant with our conditioning. The way we are brought up has either positive or negative repercussions on our thoughts. These thoughts influence our feelings or emotions. These feelings influence the way we view and relate with work, ourselves, others, and situations we come across in our lives (attitudes). Our attitudes then cause us to behave or act in a certain way. We can grow or destroy ourselves based on the way we relate with other people, situations, and life at large.

You might be thinking to yourself, "I have had these negative thoughts for so long that I find it hard to get rid of them." You might also say, "I am aware of my negative thoughts and I do all I can to get rid of them, but they keep coming back." Now you are left with this question: "How do I overcome my negative thoughts?"

In the same way that fear is dealt with, you can learn to eliminate negative thoughts. In his book titled, **Thumbs Up! Five Steps to Create the Life of Your Dreams,** Joey Reiman states, "when the fears do pop up (and they will!), we use Dr. Cohen's four R's: recognize, reject, replace and reinforce. First, *recognize* your fear. Call it out. Then *reject* it as unsound and unwarranted. Next, try to *replace* the fear with healthier, more loving thoughts. Lastly, *reinforce* your new, more nurturing thinking every day." Using the 4Rs formula repeatedly for some time, you are bound to uproot your negative thoughts and sow positive thoughts in their place. Just replace the word "fear" in the statement with the phrase "negative thoughts".

Becoming Your True Self

It is only when we learn to appreciate our uniqueness, originality, creativity, and greatness that we become our true selves. When we become our true selves we reclaim our God-given authority to be that which He created us to be. In his book called ***The Purpose and Power of Authority: Discovering the Power of Your Personal Domain,*** Myles Munroe tells us that we were all created for authority, and we are all answerable to the authority of others. Authority is what we're authorized to do by our inherent purposes. You have a God-given calling to develop your personal authority to carry out your unique purpose in life. It is only when we learn to cherish ourselves that we realize our full potential because just as John C Maxwell says, "you must know yourself to grow yourself and that you must see value in yourself to add value to yourself". We need to sit down alone and write down everything we love about ourselves. If we can have a look at our great qualities every morning and every evening, we shall cultivate and reinforce a new belief in ourselves that will have a ripple effect on our behaviors. Not only will our behaviors change, but the way we approach work and people will become healthier as well. With new thoughts, we change our emotions, and this change in our emotions impacts our attitudes, which will lead us to behave differently. Consequently, our results in life will be amazing.

I vividly recall the way I did work with my former boss and founder of TopAD Ogilvy, the late Bishop Patricia Pindeni. She was a woman of substance - strong, brave, witty, and shrewd in the way she managed her businesses. She used to make us work until late in the night whenever there was a crucial project to be managed. We did this to meet the deadlines. We would put our heads together, brainstorming on great ideas to tackle the challenge at hand. This process would often take us into the wee hours of the next day. Such was the approach we took to problem-solving. Weekends did not count if we were to deliver the best results for our clients' problems.

One Saturday morning, a sunny and beautiful day, I had to go to work to close on a difficult project with my workmates. This was soon after returning from our honeymoon with my dear and beloved wife, Tamanda. Nothing else mattered but our closeness. We were cherishing our love life. With these sweet and precious moments in my mind, I had promised to see her at lunch and as a result, had chosen not to take breakfast with her. She bade me farewell and promised me a great lunch on my return; little did I know the time I would be back. We commenced our brainstorming session and ideas started flowing. The process was enriching as much as it was mind-boggling. We closed on the idea generation process around midday and proceeded with the proposal writing.

Meanwhile, our boss was nowhere to be seen yet she had promised to be with us to close the project quickly. She came in later that afternoon to find us finishing the proposal writing. She then asked us to take her through the proposal, and she was not satisfied with our work. We had to start from scratch.

We found ourselves stuck at the stage of brainstorming ideas up until 20:30 hours. Until this hour, we had not taken either lunch or supper. I took it upon myself to ask our boss to provide us with food so that we could get re-energized – always the odd one out, courageous and daring. Meanwhile, I was boiling inside because I had broken the promise I made earlier to my dear wife to return for lunch. And so, I chose not to partake in the supper that night. When my colleagues were through with their dinner, we proceeded with writing the proposal which took us to somewhere around midnight. Having finished writing the proposal, we had to take our boss through it again. She gave it a nod around 00:30 hours.

Whenever there was a challenge to be tackled by the team, I was always willing and ready to learn from such challenges. Whatever challenges came my way, I always found ways to conquer them. When we were told to work over the weekend to sort out the challenge we had, I was very happy and more than willing and excited to be part of the winning team. Because I was ready to work, I put all my thoughts and energy into the work. Regardless of missing lunch and supper, I had a positive and winning attitude and hence we managed to close on that project. Looking at life from a positive perspective has always assisted me with winning friends in both business and life in general.

This experience made me fume at the time: I had not eaten the whole day; I failed to have a great afternoon with my dear wife; but after some time, pondering on it, I learned that our boss was testing our endurance. She wanted to make us grow into strong people who could manage pressure at all times and under all circumstances. Today, I have a strong character because of that experience. Today, I cherish her as one of the people who contributed to my discovery and appreciation of self, and learning to use my gifts well.

Finally, remember that you are unique and special. While some people will be frank with you and will be ready to help you grow, there are those who, despite how good you are to them, are going to dress you down. Whatever achievement you realize in life, they will find a way to belittle you and confuse you along your way to greatness. Trust me, you have already come across some of these people. They have already poisoned your mind. While you are fixed on your goal, you find yourself distracted by their comments. They have gone to the extent of scandalizing you. Theirs is a goal of messing you up. They are not happy with your steadfastness or hunger for growth or will power. They are good at sowing seeds of negativity to see to it that you conform to their way of doing things and live an average life.

Never mind them. Be the master and architect of your own life. Tell them you appreciate whatever they think of you; accept their thinking as opinions that they are entitled to; while deep inside choose to see a hero. A legend. An achiever. Never waste your precious time justifying yourself. Rather allow your actions to prove them wrong. Be glued to your goals in life. Conquer your challenges one by one until you emerge victorious. Endurance and resilience matter when pursuing our goals in life. Adversity, distractions, or situations beyond our control will come along to make us lose our focus, but we must persist in staying focused on our goals. I like what Pope Paul VI writes, in his encyclical called **Populorum Progression** (development of peoples), concerning the need for individual responsibility in personal development: "In the design of God, every man is called upon to develop and fulfill himself, for every life is a vocation. At birth, everyone is granted, in germ, a set of aptitudes and qualities for him to bring to fruition. Their coming to maturity, which will be the result of education received from the environment and personal efforts, will allow each man to direct himself toward the destiny intended for him by his Creator. Endowed with intelligence and freedom, he is responsible for his fulfillment as he is for his salvation. He is aided, or sometimes impeded, by those who educate him and those with whom he lives, but each one remains, whatever be these influences affecting him, the principal agent of his own success or failure. By the unaided effort of his own intelligence and his will, each man can grow in humanity, can enhance his personal worth, can become more a person."

What challenges have you come across in your life? And how did you deal with them? As long as we are human beings and still living, we should expect that challenges will come our way and hit us from left to right. But what we do after those terrible experiences, influenced by our thoughts, determines whether we are going to develop and realize our greatness or die naturally because we felt we were completely done. Here are examples of how some of our friends dealt with adversity having been beaten below the belt.

In his book titled - ***Failing Forward: Turning Mistakes into Stepping Stones for Success,*** John C Maxwell, when discussing how the past impacts the present, writes about "one man who is born with severe disabilities and decides the world owes him, while another (such as Roger Crawford) goes on to become a tennis pro. One person who contracts AIDS bitterly gives up, while another (such as basketball's Magic Johnson) builds his business and enjoys his family life. One woman experiences rape and withdraws into herself, while another (such as Kelly McGillis) overcomes the experience and becomes a successful actress in Hollywood." No matter how dark a person's past is, it need not color his present permanently. Your past is not the final statement about your future and your birthplace is not your destiny.

When I embarked on this project of writing a book, a new challenge that I had never thought of, crept up. I had our offices closed for the late payment of office rentals. This was a distraction to my book writing. This came about due to late payment from our clients. The political unrest, caused by the elections body declaring a winner while the case was in court, led the masses to take to the streets protesting against the results. The demonstrations caused havoc and business came to a standstill, with most being forced to tread carefully. With such circumstances at hand, many businesses did not realize sales as planned and hence they chose to lay off some of their personnel, postpone payments to their suppliers, and even reduce their advertising spend. This had a ripple effect on our company. We found ourselves in a quagmire and hence our failure to pay our office rentals on time. People started spreading rumors that our company had closed down and that it would no longer operate. Friends and the public at large became curious, and phone call after phone call came in to find out from me whether what they were hearing was true.

While this situation prevailed, I chose to stay focused on my goal - book writing. I managed to progress well with my new skill because I chose to remain calm despite the office closure. I chose to wait at home for our payments while I put all my energy and attention to writing this book. I chose to inspire others through this project. The point I am bringing forward to you is that any challenge you come across in life can become a stepping stone to achieving greater dreams if you remain calm, and stay focused on your goal. I am no different from you. I feel pain and hurt as you do, but I chose to be myself and placed all my energies on a new challenge while waiting to resolve my office rental issue. You, too, might find yourself discouraged by tough economic situations or something else beyond your control. Do not despair and accept defeat. Never quit! We've all heard of Henry Ford—the great automobile innovator and entrepreneur. What a lot of people don't know is that before he became famous for his automobile and $5 workday, he was a debtor who filed for bankruptcy twice. You are stronger than you think you are. You are great, you are special, and you are unique. If others did it, why can't you? You are a conqueror. You are invincible. You are a winner. Look at the giant inside you and ask for courage, resilience, and strength to reach your destiny. Empowered with these three, no one will stop you from achieving your goals. Cherish yourself. Stay focused. You are destined for victory.

Always remember that, "*Tough times never last, but tough people do.*" (Robert H Schuller). You are one of the toughest people ever created. Believe it and take it as gospel truth. Never lose your fire because of other people's opinions. Rekindle it, let it shine your way to greatness. In his book **Law of Pain**, John C Maxwell indicates that good management of bad experiences leads to great growth. Also, John McDonnel observed that "every problem introduces a person to himself."

To conclude this chapter, remember that you and I are created for greatness. You and I are meant to live our life in full. However, our greatness is either achieved or lost depending on our thoughts. Remember that our thoughts can either build or destroy us completely. We are, therefore, expected to remain watchful and vigilant to ensure that we cultivate positive thoughts and uproot negative ones. Whatever thoughts we allow into our minds have an effect on our feelings, and in turn, our feelings affect our attitudes. These attitudes, then influence the way we behave and our behaviors make up our habits. We must be careful then that we grow up with amazing and great thoughts that will help us win friends and therefore grow our businesses and our professional careers.

In the next chapter, you shall come across the importance of asking pertinent and intelligent questions. The more questions you have in your mind, the more time you spend on seeking answers to those questions. While some answers can be found from the people around you, whether your seniors at work, elders in the village, or professors at universities, others will require that you read volumes and volumes of books to come across them. It is now the moment that we resuscitate the child within us to help ask more and more questions until we quench our thirst for the truth. Hence, in this chapter you shall see and learn the power of wonder and of asking questions. Turn to the next page.

Chapter Seven

DO YOU KNOW THE ROLE OF QUESTIONS IN YOUR LIFE?

*"Ask yourself an interesting enough question and
your attempt to find a tailor-made solution to that
question will push you to a place where, pretty soon,
you'll find yourself all by your lonesome – which I
think is a more interesting place to be."*
– Chuck Close

Life is the greatest teacher of all time. It teaches each one of us unique lessons and takes us through unique examinations, through challenges and problems. Also note that no two individuals are given the same examination. Life appreciates whatever answers you give to the examination questions received. What's important, however, is not life's questions nor our answers but rather whether we get out of the examination room transformed, the same or frustrated. The ball remains in your court to make that choice. Tell me, thus far how have you come out of life's exam room?

Remember, only you are in charge of your life. So why not make lemonade if given lemons by your examiner? I can tell you now that whining does not help. When challenges arise, that is when you need to engage in asking yourself questions; probing open-ended questions that make you sweat, but that by the time you are done responding to them, offer you tremendous transformation within. Sometimes you need to face yourself in the mirror and ask yourself open-ended questions. We as a people tend to run away from asking ourselves questions. Why? We are afraid to face ourselves, and yet again, the reason being that our questioning spirit was killed as we grew up while attending school. We are afraid to venture into any unknown territory, yet it is in being free with ourselves to get into this foreign land that we find what we are meant to achieve in life. It is through the spirit of risking it all by facing ourselves through these questions that we liberate ourselves. By frequently asking ourselves open-ended questions, questions like the following I found in a book titled, ***A More Beautiful Question: The Power of Inquiry to Spark Breakthrough Ideas,*** *by* Warren Berger, we end up liberating ourselves and living our dream life:

- Why am I not happy? (And what if I were to do something about that?)

- Is there a different question I should be asking?

- Why am I asking why?

- When we step back, what do we then see?

- Why did the idea/effort fail? What if I could take what I've learned from this failure and try a revised approach? How might I do that?

- Why should I believe you when you tell me something can't be done?

- What if you sleep with a question? Will you wake up with an answer?

- How do I learn to learn from failure?

In this book, Warren Berger states that one of the most important things questioning does is to enable people to think and act in the face of uncertainty. New ideas arise from us when we engage in questioning the status quo. Without us questioning the way things are done and even the way we think, we cannot realize our dreams. The more you and I ask questions or never settle for less, the more innovative we become. With innovation comes the introduction of new products or services and even switching of careers from current to new ones; and this effectively leads to internal growth and finally, living our dream life. We can only break the chains of the status quo if we engage our minds in asking questions. What questioning, or an inquisitive spirit, does is to assist you to stay strong and open-minded to the possibilities for change, and prepares you to face life's challenges head-on and as a result, become transformed for the better. This is the only prerequisite for excellence.

In the same book, I came across this question that intrigued me the most, "What kind of preparation does the modern workplace and society demand of its citizens? -i.e. what kind of skills, knowledge, and capabilities are needed to be productive and thrive?" Thinking about and giving an answer to this question is not easy. I bet we agree that this is a difficult question to answer. In this book, Warren Berger writes that the answer to that, again, is not simple, but among those who've studied the needs of the evolving workplace from an educational standpoint - and two people at the forefront are Tony Wagner and John Seely Brown - the consensus seems to be that this new world demands citizens who are **self-learners**; who are **creative** and **resourceful**; who can **adjust** and **adapt** to **constant change**. Both Wagner and Brown put "**questioning**" at the top of the key survival skills for the new marketplace. Now, if you can do some introspection, when did you last read a book that taught you something new and profound? If your response to this question is that you have read none, you put yourself in jeopardy. Sooner or later you will surely find yourself irrelevant or redundant as the workplace and society keep on changing. And when such a situation arises, who will you blame?

Different People, Same Script

You would probably agree with me that most times when you meet people, they will tell you a similar story: 'Mfwetu, boetie, all is not well man. These politicians have absolutely messed us up. We are screwed boetie. Nothing is working. Hey man, I don't know what to do next!' Those are the sentiments of most people today. We have reached a point where we refuse to challenge our brain to think beyond the norm. Even the brain itself is deceiving us to take the road most traveled - the easy way out. Why? Instead of challenging the status quo, we have chosen to accept it as the only way to live. When our conscious mind starts to question the status quo, the subconscious quickly comes in to twist it into never delving deeper into finding answers that can unleash our potential. Instead, it encourages us to remain subservient to the subconscious. This influences the conscious mind to follow a routine and ignore facing any challenge. However, we forget that nothing worth pursuing ever comes easy. Living on autopilot is dangerous. It takes us nowhere except in circles until we return to where we started from. Year in and year out, we do the same things expecting different results: the definition of insanity. We need to start doing things differently.

The Solution

When we reach a point where we see things not making sense or adding up, we need to stop and start asking ourselves serious questions. That is the moment when we need to do a serious soul search. Why? It is when we resurrect the genius in us. This is the time to awaken the giant within and allow it to guide and lead us in a different direction, onto another path.

> *"There are certain lessons in life that have to be learned the hard way. Eventually you realize the painful experiences turn into wisdom. They were needed in order to show you your true inner strength. You may stumble, and you may even fall…**but never let anything stop you from getting back up.**"*
> – Unknown

I had all it takes to be happy being a child brought up and raised in a rich family in town. My happiness was short-lived though, as my dad and mum separated. This led me to experience a new life in the village. One thing I noticed, though young, was that my mum, my siblings, and myself were not welcome in the village. We were denied by our blood, our relatives. It was such a shame. The moment I noticed this hatred, questions started flowing through my mind. Why are these people full of hatred? What crime have we committed? Why are we seen as outcasts by our very own relatives? Questions, yes questions kept on coming. I was interested in digging for the truth behind that hatred.

I went to school and performed well. They continued hating me. They said, "Who does he think he is? He will achieve nothing but conform to village life. Leave him. He will soon be like us." They kept on hurting me with their words; adding salt on a fresh wound. However, I chose to think and act differently. I was defiant. Inside me was a young man who said to himself, 'Prove them wrong, you don't belong here.' I was relentless in the pursuit of my goals. To their dismay, I made it to where I dreamt of being while they watched.

In town, I successfully worked for various companies, but I was never satisfied. My jobs did not give me the challenge I was looking for and I became disgruntled. As usual, I engaged in monologues. I started asking myself questions: Why am I doing this? Is there any joy in it? What else can I do that can give me the joy I am looking for? Is this all I have? Question after question kept on coming. A moment came when I told myself enough was enough. I resigned from a great job and got myself a new job in a foreign country, South Africa. Did I end up going to work in Egoli, the City of Gold? No, something else came up.

While my new employer was sorting out my work permit to move me to Johannesburg, my former employer messed up a big account. An account that my new employer guarded so jealously that they did not want to lose. The owner of this business informed my new employer that no one else in Malawi could handle that account except me when they had a chat about the way forward. This posed a challenge to both my new employer and myself. My new employer then challenged me with two options: one to work on a contract in Johannesburg and the other, to start my own company that they would support in its infancy. Questions came, and they kept on coming up in my mind. Questions like; of these two options, which one is best for me? What are the pros and cons of each option? How will I arrive at the best option? And what will be the consequences of my choice? It was indeed a challenging time. My decision-making capabilities were challenged, but, as usual, being a fighter at heart, I challenged myself for answers until I reached my verdict.

This is the time where I had to revisit the child in me for answers, the giant sleeping within me, that I believed had the right answers to my challenge. While deep in introspection, I recalled myself being an achiever, great, and living my dream life. I remembered and unearthed one of my childhood dreams; a dream of becoming my own boss, running my own company. This option came out on top over the other. Why was it my number one option? Because it was in sync with my purpose. My purpose, I had learned, was to reach out and help people realize their dreams. Being my own boss meant that I could make money; money that would help me assist those in need. Making a difference in people's lives meant and still means a lot to me. Yes, this option augured well with my dream.

But before I could give my new employer my response, I needed to engage in a serious discussion with my better half and only confidante, Sekani. Why? When I had found the new job in Johannesburg, I shared with her the great news and she was exhilarated. Her eyes were on the City of Gold. I had to find a way of discussing the challenge we had. I told her that if we chose to go and work in Johannesburg, we would rise and reach the peak easily, but then, once the contract was terminated, we would have to get back to square one. However, if I could start my own company, we would start from the ground, then we would grow and never get back to square one. I further asked her to think about it for three days. Are you curious to learn what her response was? Obviously yes, I can see it in your eyes, you are. She said to me, "Bob, my dear husband, follow your heart. Take the risk and start your company. I am here to support you." See all of us need the support of our dear wives and husbands to excel in life. Yes, all we need is a little help to excel in life.

Later on, I gave my new employer feedback about my final option. They congratulated me on taking the bold step rarely taken by most people. I had no money, but I had my instinct, skills, and expertise. I had no money but I did have connections, people, or friends whom Les Brown refers to as OQP (only quality people). Believing the awakened giant in me helped me make it. From one client my business grew to manage several big local and multinational clients. All this happened because I allowed the child in me to lead the way. His inquisitiveness allowed me to be on top of the game. Questions, and great questions at questioning myself, helped me along the journey. While I had the opportunity to use the road many people travel, I chose to take my life down the road less traveled.

> *"Believe in yourself and all that you are. Know that*
> *there is something inside you that is greater than*
> *any obstacle."*
> **– Christian D Larson**

Is it going to be easy? No. Is it going to be tough? Yes. You shall surely stumble along the way. You will fail greatly, but never give up. Failure is the stepping stone to greatness. Make mistakes as much as you can and learn from these mistakes in order to proceed with your itinerary to greatness.

I, too, have made my own mistakes. I have made a lot of them in the course of running my business, and have also learned from them. I am courageous, focused, resilient, and strong because I chose to focus on my goals while learning from my mistakes. Yes, I have encountered distractors - a lot of them - but not a single day did I give up. I have always believed in the child inside of me, the giant within. Life is beautiful when you encounter stumbling blocks along the way. Facing the challenges head-on, dismantling them, and conquering them gives us a sense of satisfaction. Without challenges, life would be meaningless. We are made to challenge ourselves and move on. Challenges are opportunities and sparks that ignite the fire in us to conquer the world. Set-backs are, in fact, setups. The bigger the challenges, the greater the victories if you focus on your goal, and if you are open to learning from every moment of your life.

The moment you and I come face to face with the child in us is the moment we find ourselves achieving the unimaginable. The moment we allow the child within to ask those great questions is the moment our life takes a new twist. It is the moment we realize our dreams and live life to the fullest. I want to encourage you to take time to question the status quo. Take time to challenge yourself. Take time to stretch your thinking. Move out of the comfort zone to discover yourself. There is a giant inside you that is sleeping. Awaken him. Allow him to lead you to greatness. You are special, you are original and you are unique.

Remember that society reprogrammed you to be what you are now. The new you. Your false alibi. Not your original self. Society encouraged the giant within you to stay asleep all this time. Awaken this giant within and live life to the fullest. Meditate on this powerful statement:

> *"Beliefs have the power to create and the power to destroy. Human beings have the awesome ability to take any experience of their lives and create a meaning that disempowers them or one that can literally save their lives."*
> **– Tony Robbins**

Question everything you have learned over the course of your life so far - from your childhood until now. Leave no stone unturned. Question your culture - is it real? Why did your ancestors come up with such a culture or an approach to life? What about the beliefs that this culture follows? Why did they want you to learn these beliefs? Why were they important? Are they relevant now?

Remember, your beliefs are learned from the people you have rubbed shoulders with and from the society you have lived in. Again, beliefs, having been learned, are not fixed, they can be unlearned. All the more reason you and I should constantly find ourselves questioning ourselves. The more we engage ourselves in questioning everything, the better informed we become. Your living life on your terms depends largely on asking questions. I challenge you to never be satisfied with the status quo but keep asking questions until you find your truth. Heroes and legends, to make all those discoveries that we are happy to have learned, had time to themselves. Time to ask themselves questions. They took a step back in life and asked themselves vital questions. They relentlessly asked themselves profound questions that gave them profound answers. They never believed what they learned during their lifetime. If you and I keep on asking questions, we too shall live a great life. We too shall leave an impact on this world.

Finally, in summary, you and I have learned that our creativity is resuscitated the moment we step back and ask ourselves open-ended questions. We have noted that if we remain children, always asking ourselves questions, we end up living our dream life. See now, how important it is to question everything? Yes, now that we have learned the impact of questioning in our life, we must engage more than ever before in constantly asking ourselves questions. Questioning will lead us to dig for answers. These answers we find in either the books we read or search engines like Google and other online resource centers.

In the next chapter, you are going to understand the importance of living a life based on the decisions you make. A life that depends on the power inside you, not one that is influenced by external forces. Who is influencing your decision-making? Is it yourself, or others? Hence, you and I must live our life based on the decisions we make ourselves. Let's go to the next chapter and learn more.

Chapter Eight

DECISIONS: WHO INFLUENCES THE DECISIONS YOU MAKE?

"I'm slowly learning that even if I react, it won't change anything, it won't make people suddenly love and respect me, it won't magically change their minds. Sometimes it's better to just let things be, let people go, don't fight for closure, don't ask for explanations, don't chase answers and don't expect people to understand where you are coming from. I'm slowly learning that life is better lived when you don't center it on what's happening around you and center it on what's happening inside you instead. Work on yourself and your inner peace."
– Unknown

Who Influences Your Decisions? Yourself or Others?

What makes you tick? What influences the decisions you make? And who influences the decisions you make? You might be wondering why I have asked you these three probing questions. I am interested in making you aware of yourself. You must know yourself fully to live your life in full. Bear in mind that some people are led by their big dreams in life while others go with the crowd - whatever comes their way makes them tick. Each one of us is driven by either our purpose or the day dictates what we should do to arrive at a decision. Some people have a sense of control; they are the masters of their own game; they plan their day in advance with all the activities for the day laid out on paper; while others are led by other people to live their life, being told what to do every day. Which group of people do you belong to? The one in charge of all the things happening around them - the one living from the cause side of the *cause and effect equation* - or the other one that wakes up every day to be told what to do - the one living from the effect side of the equation?

You need to understand that the level of autonomy you have (being yourself under any circumstance), determines the level of freedom you have in decision making and at the same time the ability to achieve your dream life. While it is true that in life we need people to excel in whatever business or profession we are engaged in, we also need the ability to make our decisions independently to live our life in full. The more reason you and I need to be aware of the factors that influence our decision making. Are these factors internal or external? What are these internal factors that affect us as we make decisions? Achievement, dreams, drive, purpose, self-efficacy, self-knowledge, self-worth, sense of direction? And what are the external forces that influence our decisions? Culture, education, family, friends, people, peers, circumstances, work, political, economic, social, and technological factors? These two forces put pressure on us every time we are making decisions in life. All the more reason you and I need to know that we have an inherent power within reach to control anything under any circumstance. We must get out of the cocoon and realize this power within us.

Our life is, to a great extent, the feedback we have received from the people we have mostly interacted with and are still interacting with. The people who molded us during our childhood, the ones who shared their dreams and fears with us during our adolescence, young adulthood, and old age have, at some point, said something that we thought made great sense. This we kept in our subconscious mind. On another note, some people have made comments about us that have influenced our life either positively or negatively. Again, these comments were also stored in our subconscious mind. An unknown author once said, "In life you will meet two kinds of people. Ones who build you up, and ones who tear you down. But in the end, you will thank them both." These two types of people are worth knowing and taking note of. Why? While some people are to be cherished and nurtured as friends by us, because they have our well-being at heart, there are also others who, no matter how great our dreams are, will destroy them before they are hatched. These we must, at all costs, relate with cautiously. Some people are there to see us grow and realize our dreams. They celebrate our successes. Others are there to make sure that no matter what, you and I never achieve our dreams, but live an average life. Our interactions with these people leave lasting impressions on our subconscious mind, whether we like it or not. We react to situations and circumstances differently based on the experiences we have had with these two types of people. The fact of life is these people are with us for the long haul, whether we like it or not, for as long as we are alive.

We do find within us the adventurous, risk-taking, and the 'I don't care' spirited personality on the one hand, while on the other, is the weak, fearsome, and risk-averse personality. Why? It is because of people's influences exerting pressure on us. Can we run away from these pressures? No. Can we control them? Yes. Totally. Whoever we allow to influence our decisions in life has no or little control over us. We are in total control. We decide whether to be happy or not, whether to work or not, whether to react positively or negatively in any situation. The onus is on us. However, despite us being in total control of our situations, some of us will express control over the circumstances we find ourselves in, while others will need the input of other people to assist them to overcome the situations they encounter in life. Rubbing shoulders with these people is unavoidable as long as we live. We shall keep encountering both positive and negative people. These people, directly or indirectly, will affect our way of life whether we like it or not. With their comments, we can either soar high and realize our greatness, or we can look down upon ourselves and hit the bottom low. It all depends on us; the ball is in our court. Are we a people influenced by external forces or internal ones? Do we live our lives inside out or outside in?

Where Do You Gain Your Power? External or Internal?

People who live their life outside in are greatly influenced by external forces; they are conformists. They live from the effect side of the *cause and effect equation*. They look for a reason as to why things happened the way they did. There are a lot of external forces, that if not careful, can impact these people negatively. And once they do, these people are in for it. Because of their tendency to believe what they are told by their friends, family, colleagues at work, and other social gatherings, these people tend to look forward to receiving their approval in whatever they find themselves engaged in. These people always inform others of what they are up to and they expect them to pat them on the back for pursuing whatever they have chosen to do. Comments from others either build them up or destroy them completely depending on what they say to them. Because these people have chosen to be influenced by the comments of their friends and family, they tend to be emotionally immature. With emotional immaturity, any negative comment received has a terrible ripple effect on them. They become easily wounded, they think people don't appreciate their contributions, and in the end, they become frustrated all the time. Eventually, their output becomes less than they could achieve. They become less productive than they are meant to be, and they relate negatively with other people. Fewer friends imply fewer connections which leads to believing less in themselves. A negative belief leads to less effort and eventually minimal output. Eventually, they resort to leading an average life.

On the other hand, people who are influenced by internal forces, live their life inside out. These are non-conformists. These are carefree people who couldn't care less about what people say about them. They cause things to happen. They are influenced by their own self-drive and have a sense of direction. Regardless of whatever people say about them, they put their focus on their goals. These people know what they want to achieve in life and they put plans in place to achieve whatever they have set their eyes on. They are never disturbed by external influences. They can only analyze the external forces to make sure that they remain on course with their goals. Because they are focused, they can easily adjust themselves to take into account the effects of the external forces on their journey in life. These people are emotionally mature. They don't go out to seek the approval of friends and family. They dictate the terms of their life. They are in total control. Being in control helps them achieve a lot in life. With great achievements, they tend to be happy people. They live life on their terms and tend to ignore influences from their friends and family unless their influence is positive and adds value. They never believe anything their friends and family say about them that would take them out of their blessings and dreams. They question the motive behind what their friends say about them. In the end, they make informed choices having sieved the comments given. These people tend to be the happiest, most adventurous, and risk-takers. Because of their willingness to take risks, they are ready to make mistakes and learn from them. In the process, they are continuously learning and improving themselves. Such an approach to life leads them to achieve awesome results.

My challenge to you is to answer the question: what type of person are you? A conformist or non-conformist?

Are You a Conformist or a Non-Conformist?

If you are a conformist, do not despair, you can turn the tables upside down. It all depends on you. There are remedies to assist you to become a non-conformist, a carefree personality. You can join the non-conformists and live your dream life. You have lived this average life because of your way of seeing things. You can be assisted to see the world from a different perspective and become the best in the world. You need to be trained into seeing the world from a different perspective; to challenge the status quo. To get a glimpse of what the status quo represents, have a look at the "**11 Ways to be Unremarkably Average**" list below. This list I came across while reading a book titled ***The Art of Non-Conformity – Set Your Own Rules, Live the Life You Want and Change the World***, by Chris Guillebeau. He further states that this list and its variations represent a safe, comfortable life. "The list is not complete, and you could probably add a few items to it based on your own experiences or those of other people you know", he emphasizes.

11 Ways to be Unremarkably Average

1. Accept what people tell you at face value.
2. Don't question authority.
3. Go to college because you are supposed to, not because you want to learn something.
4. Go overseas once or twice in your life, to somewhere safe like

England.

5. Don't try to learn another language, everyone else will eventually learn English.

6. Think about starting your own business, but never do it.

7. Think about writing a book, but never do it.

8. Get the largest mortgage you qualify for and spend 30 years paying for it.

9. Sit at a desk 40 hours a week for an average of 10 hours of productive work.

10. Don't stand out or draw attention to yourself.

11. Jump through hoops. Check off boxes.

You need to change your beliefs, attitudes, emotions, thoughts, and behavior. It is the journey that starts from within that will see you become a non-conformist. As challenging as this journey may be, the results of embarking on it are great. Imagine seeing yourself become a carefree personality, having lived most of your life a conformist. How happy will you be? You are made to make a difference in life. Why settle for less? There are people around who lived exactly the way you are living, but they had to change their way of thinking to become non-conformists. It's doable and achievable. Never allow yourself to only exist - you were made to live. Bury yourself in books you never read while at school and learn from them. Browse and watch videos on YouTube and see how fast you can see the fruits of your labor.

Non-conformists enjoy life to the fullest. They spend most of their time improving themselves through continuous learning. These people are always curious. These people have awakened the giant within themselves. They have allowed the child within them to take the lead. They are risk-takers and adventurous. They mind their own business and will have nothing to do with whatever people say about them. Non-conformists do not believe in the status quo, but instead, question everything in life. They even question the way they think. They analyze their thoughts. They challenge themselves and rely on the power inside them. They hit a blank wall, fall, and rise again. They are in charge of their life and laugh at their own mistakes. They see life as a game to play, the results of which are either winning or learning. With such an approach to life, these people venture into businesses that flourish. Change yourself now by taking that bold step: the step that will make you leave that miserable life and step into greatness. Into a new world where comments from other people matter the least. The world of zoning in on yourself.

Several techniques are at your disposal to help you become a non-conformist. Much as there are always several options or strategies that can be used to reach a destination, so too are there several strategies to change the way you think to become a non-conformist. You can either choose to walk, run, ride a bicycle, drive a car, travel by road or rail or air to arrive wherever you intend to go. Equally, you can either train yourself or engage other people to transform the way you think or perceive the world, to become a non-conformist. To choose an option that can take you to the promised land, there are several factors you must consider first.

1. Choice

One of these factors is choice. We are at liberty to choose whether we intend to become the best in the world or live mediocre lives. It all depends on our internal voice. Is this internal voice telling us to be satisfied with the status quo or is it challenging us to act differently? Change is a choice that each one of us must opt for to get us to where we intend to be from where we are. We cannot see ourselves improving with the same approach we have had all our life. That's insanity at its best. We can only realize our dreams if we engage in new strategies or use a different approach to life. Do we realize we have the choice at our disposal? Are we willing to make a choice that will make us better people? A choice that will see us achieve great results, unlike the ones we have so far achieved. We are the deciders of the type of life we intend to live. We are at liberty to free ourselves or imprison ourselves, to live a happy life or a miserable one. What choice are you willing to make? You are the captain of your ship of life, and no one else is but you. Be bold and make that choice now to live a happy and fulfilled life.

2. Pleasure or Pain

Another factor that affects us is pleasure or pain. As human beings, we are naturally driven either towards pleasure or away from pain to achieve whatever we want in life. The pleasure derived from our efforts for greatness, and attaining that greatness, drives or motivates us to work towards achieving feats that are unheard of. We work amazingly hard and smart to make sure that we realize our dream no matter what, as long as we anticipate the joy that will come from such an achievement. On another note, the pain we feel from the state we are in drives us towards achieving greatness. Painful experiences cause us to be uncomfortable with our current status. Due to these painful experiences, we work hard to move away from pain and achieve greatness. The more reason pain sometimes also plays a great role in pushing us to work relentlessly for a new cause.

These two factors, pleasure or pain, play a great role in motivating us to realize our dreams. What is it that you are aspiring to achieve? And what pleasure are you anticipating to enjoy? Or what painful experience are you going through now that you want to make sure you eliminate? You are in charge of your life, and no one can have power over you. You have within you an ace card that can either empower or break you. You are a fighter, yes, a fighter that always wins. Stay focused, release the power in you to win all your battles. Greatness is a challenge and needs people who are relentless in their pursuit of goals. Those who are not persistent never make it.

3.   Seeing Life as an Adventure

Explore life and enjoy it while you can. Allow yourself to be adventurous. Visit those places you have always wanted to visit. Travel the world to see new places and faces. Let your dream come true. It is your own life - live it on your terms. Ignore whatever the people you rub shoulders with say about your dreams. Some might believe in your dreams while others won't. You are the driver of your bus. Never look back and never doubt yourself. Aim high and take the necessary steps to achieve your goals. Be relentless. Make mistakes, learn from them, and push on. Then keep pushing on some more. It is only when you constantly work on improving yourself that you will attain your dreams.

4.   Fear

Fear is another factor that either inspires us for greatness or destroys us completely. While there are many types of fear, I am very familiar with the fear of heights and public speaking. I may not be the only one who has had a fear of public speaking and that of heights. You, too, might be among the people who are bothered with these two. If you are like me, what are you doing to overcome these fears? These two types of fear have haunted me a lot in my life. These two have had both a positive and negative impact on me. What are your most common fears? How are you dealing with these fears?

You might have great dreams; seeing yourself living an amazing life, but when fear sets in, all these thoughts for greatness scatter. Instead, the fear leaves us shaking and sweating profusely. What are you doing to face your fears head-on? Either you tell yourself enough is enough and you get out of your cocoon to combat your fears to free yourself, or you keep on accepting these fears and live an average life. Fear is natural and we can never part ways with it. Fear is what has driven most heroes and heroines to reach heights never reached before. All they did was to manage their fear so they could realize their dreams. Fear of failure is necessary for we work hard to prove a point - that we are achievers. Do not allow fear to swat your dreams. Let fear drive you to greatness. Let fear make you a hero or heroine.

As I said earlier on, I have been haunted by two types of fear - that of public speaking and heights. With the awareness of these two types of fear and their impact on my life, I had to make a bold decision. A decision that assisted me to conquer my fears. Bear in mind that I had goals I lived by. One of them was to become a professional speaker, yet I was stuck in fear of public speaking. This was one of the burning desires of my life; to use my voice to change the way people think about and see themselves. Being a burning desire, I had to rise up and find a way of managing my fear of public speaking. If you want to learn to swim, you don't read books about swimming to become a swimmer, you have to dive into the water. Drown and get rescued time and again, until you make it. Equally, I had to join the Toastmasters International club to learn public speaking and leadership skills. Today, I speak fluently and easily in public because I chose to live above my fear. I urge you to assess yourself and find out the fears you have. The fears that are stopping you from realizing your dream.

Are you interested in getting to know how I defeated my fear of heights? My gut feeling tells me you are. Why? You too are keen to overcome your fears. Living with the fear of heights, I had another desire - to climb Mulanje Mountain. This is the third largest mountain in the Southern part of Africa. There were speculations that people who climbed this mountain never returned because it was dangerous to get to the highest peak. Stories of people who got lost after attempting to climb this mountain were fresh in the minds of people. However, despite these stories, I had the nerve to climb this mountain as a way of conquering my fear of heights.

While home, one afternoon, I was going through my Facebook page and a post caught my attention. My colleague, Agness Mizere, had written a story about a very good guide when it came to climbing Mulanje Mountain. His contact details were there in her post. Immediately I copied and saved this gentleman's contacts on my phone. His name is Snowden Phiri.

The next thing I did was to call Snowden to find out when the right time to climb the mountain was. He told me that then was the right time to climb it. Thinking about his response left me captivated. I wondered why then was the best time to climb the mountain and I asked him. He informed me that it was the best time because in January the mountain is covered by clouds, and the fact that it was the beginning of the rainy season, gave us a great opportunity to cover a long distance and slippery places with ease. I promptly asked him the necessities required for this adventure to come true. He sent me a list and *sine dubio* (without a doubt), I transferred funds into his account to allow him to prepare for our adventure on 18th January 2018 in good time. I told my dear wife, Sekani, about this trip and she just said, "You are such a naughty man. Why do you act like this? You just follow whatever your gut feeling tells you." After a playful reprimand, she then encouraged me to take the trip and wished me the best of luck.

On 18th January 2018, a surprisingly cold morning, I woke up early, got ready, and called my uncle, Justin Dzanjalimodzi. He was accompanying me on this adventure. He confirmed that he was also ready. I drove out of our home to pick him from Blantyre Sports Club before heading to Mulanje. Around 07:00 hours, we found ourselves in Mulanje, Likhubula CCAP, where we were to meet our tour guide. Upon disembarking from the car, I called Snowden to inform him that we had arrived at our meeting point. He came and greeted us. Here we were to climb one of the largest mountains in Africa, Mulanje Mountain. Our tour guide took us through the details of our journey up the mountain. He told us that two routes are used to climb the mountain; the skyline which was tough, difficult and shorter, and another path which was longer and easy route to reach the first top part of the mountain. He then asked us which of the two routes we were comfortable with, and we chose the skyline.

By 08:00 hours, the three of us commenced the journey up the mountain. Hell broke loose when my uncle told us that he was not proceeding with us on this journey. The ascent was really tough, but I challenged him. He eventually gave in and we continued with the journey. Was it easy? No. Tough? Absolutely!

Through periods of rest and climbing on, we covered 25km in seven hours to reach Chisepo Hut, where we spent a night before proceeding to Sapitwa., Sapitwa is the highest peak of the mountain, standing at 3002m above sea level. It rained cats and dogs that night, and our dream of reaching the highest peak was swatted by this rain. Our guide told us it becomes dangerous to climb this part of the mountain with the rains. This news made me sad, and I felt frustrated that we could not make it to the peak.

Morning came, however, and our guide told us that the weather was brilliant for the next challenge. This news pumped me up with lots of energy. My uncle, him, and I started the ascent to Sapitwa Peak which was 3.5km from this hut. This was the most difficult and dangerous part of our adventure. We kept on climbing and passed through caves three times until we reached the peak. I was exhilarated! I was the happiest man on the 19th of January 2018, the moment I set my feet on Sapitwa. It took us six hours to reach this peak. I shouted on top of my voice, "Eureka! Yes, I have made it!" All I could see while there were clouds as the day was foggy. Descending the mountain was now the most dangerous part of our journey, but we eventually made it. It is on that mountain peak where I conquered my fear of heights.

What did I learn from conquering both my fear of public speaking and that of heights? If we challenge ourselves to overcome whatever fears we have and set out to conquer those fears, we will surely become victors. We will come out victorious and happy for our feat. Resilience and taking necessary steps to conquer our fears allow us to achieve our goals no matter what. You too can conquer your fears. Do it now so you can realize and live your dream life. You are the master of the course of your life. Be a non-conformist and live life on your terms. Remember that you matter. Live dangerously and be adventurous. That way you shall have lived your life to the fullest.

5.   Self-Doubt

Finally, self-doubt kills us before our actual and real death. We can have great and brilliant ideas; ideas that can lead us to greatness. We can desire to leave an impact in this world, but when doubt sets in, be assured that everything else tumbles down. It is really bad to doubt ourselves and our capabilities. We are created to live our life to the fullest so why doubt? Why not believe in ourselves? A life of greatness and living life on our terms requires that we believe in ourselves no matter what. We might see ourselves as failures due to our upbringing, our experiences in life, and a failure to understand some ideas, but that does not mean we cannot achieve anything in life.

When we have doubts about ourselves, we need to engage in questions that can empower us. Questions that will see us overcome our self-doubts. You and I are made to realize great results. You and I are made to conquer the world and ourselves to live the dream life. I recall back then when I was a little boy, 11 years old, how my uncle referred to me as a very useless boy who was up to nothing. He said that I was unruly and uncultured. This encounter with him not only made me furious but caused me to look down on myself. I ended up asking myself questions like, "How could he call me such names? And what are his motives?" Later on, after I had cooled down, I told myself that I would prove him wrong. Today, I am one of his favorite nephews having overcome the odds.

Sit down and make time to assess yourself. Are you strong or easily broken? What influences your decisions and who is behind the decisions you make? What type of people do you spend most of your time with? Are these people worthy of your time or not? What impact do they have in your realization of the dreams you have? Or are they there to discourage you from achieving them? Are you influenced by the power within you or the people and circumstances around you? You matter the most. Stay away from toxic people with negative energy. Cherish those that encourage and support your dreams and never settle for less.

In summary, our upbringing and the experiences we have had in life do impact our decision making. These experiences give us the spectacles through which we look at and interpret all reality. Depending on how we interpret the circumstances and experiences we come across, we either become conformists or non-conformists. Also remember that choice, pain or pleasure, adventure, fear, and self-doubt also have an impact on us. How we manage these forces can allow us to live a great life or an average one. The choice is yours as you are the captain of your ship.

In the next chapter, you are going to understand why you and I need to step back, PAUSE, and find out for ourselves whether we are progressing or not. Stepping back helps us see what we have done, and how well or badly we have performed. Taking a pause brings us back on track. The pause gives us the power to forge ahead in life. Flip onto the next page for more.

Chapter Nine

THE POWER OF THE PAUSE

*"Re-set, Re-adjust, Re-start, Re-focus as many
times as you need to."*
–Unknown

Life without pausing is meaningless. A pause in life is very important. It helps us to step back and see ourselves in retrospect. A pause helps us see the distance we have covered and how much further we intend to go to reach our destiny. A pause helps us see the strides we have made and the failures we have encountered, or lessons learned. We can see the direction we can take in life to stay on course and remain focused. We can also better appreciate ourselves as humans. Pausing helps us see the areas we are very good at and those that need be improved upon if we are to stay focused and strong to actualize our dreams. It keeps us focused on the goals we set for ourselves despite all the disruptions in life. A pause keeps us determined to reach our destination no matter what and refuels us to continue with our journey; without it we may find ourselves giving up easily. It re-energizes us to keep going despite the challenges that we encounter, challenges that would otherwise make us give up had we not paused. Pausing helps us see the giant within, the one that encourages us to fight our battles until we win. A pause helps us see who we truly are and is necessary for our continuous personal improvement. We will never learn anything new without a pause. We can never make the best decisions without pausing. A pause allows us to evaluate our progress.

Why We Often Don't Pause

You would, however, agree with me that most of the time we are in a hurry. Everything around us seems to be running at a terrific speed. Digital noise and technological advances, especially the emergence of smartphones and smart TVs, have brought with them our desire to be all over the place. We are interested in being on top of our game by taking in everything that is happening around us. In the end, our attention is scattered all over, instead of being focused on one important thing at a time as we are meant to do. This tendency to rush through everything we do brings with it attention deficit disorder (ADD). We cannot stay focused on one important thing at a time for long. We have turned ourselves into people who are always multi-tasking. In his book, titled **Unlimited Memory: How to Use Advanced Learning Strategies to Learn Faster, Remember More and Be More Productive**, Grandmaster Kevin Horsley quotes a Neuroscience consultant, Marilee Springer saying, "Multitasking is known to slow people down by 50% and add 50% more mistakes." He further states that multitasking is like putting your brain on drugs. He finally says that there is a whole body of research that shows that multitasking is less productive, makes you less creative, and contributes to you making bad decisions. No wonder, by the end of the day, we find ourselves tired and stressed, with nothing tangible to point at.

Imagine yourself, early in the morning, in a car driving to work: you turn on the radio. Next, you click the buttons of your smartphone to check the posts of your friends on social media; then you attend to emails and message notifications, if not these, then it's notifications from WhatsApp and Telegram, and mind you, this is on the road. The thing is we act like a DJ or VJ on the road, who while playing great songs for his audience to enjoy, is also searching for the next best song to play. He switches his attention from playing the best song to searching for the next best song, and this goes on and on. You and myself, while driving our cars and watching whatever is happening on the road as we drive, find ourselves switching our attention to our smartphones, either responding to messages on Instagram and Twitter or watching videos sent by our friends through WhatsApp. All this happens not only on the road but also, bear in mind, this is rush hour during which everyone is in a hurry to arrive at work or business on time. If, then, we find ourselves involved in an accident, should we really be surprised? Aren't we responsible for this careless driving that leads us into accidents that we can easily avoid?

Why do we find ourselves in these positions? We want to be a jack of all trades, yet we are created to specialize in one thing at a time. We are in a hurry to meet all sorts of demands from family, friends, church, work, and even business demands. All these demands are exerting a lot of pressure on us that our sense of concentration is next to zero. Before we know it, time passes us by without realizing it. We are fired up with meeting the deadlines given by our clients and other people at the expense of our own goals, and later on our dreams. We are tied up with attending to our children's homework. We are tied up with meeting the needs of our families. We are tied up with the demands of our church. We are tied up with planning the events of our friends. We are tied up with digital noise. Before we know it, we have lost the day, the week, the month, the year, and perhaps decades.

Why? Because when we come to check what we have achieved at the end of the year, we realize that we have achieved nothing. We are driven by forces beyond our control, forces we have little or no control over. Why? We never set up time for ourselves to pause. You might accuse me of being pedantic for dwelling so much on the importance of a pause that I end up ignoring the most important issues of life. But did you know that pausing is one of the most important aspects of life? Without a pause you can end up going in circles, round and round, with zero achievements. A pause plays a great and significant role in your life. Whether you like it or not, the fact is, a pause is a **must** for each one of us to take back control over our lives and to live a fulfilled life.

> *"And so, my dearest Paulinus, tear yourself away from the crowd, and, too much storm-tossed for the time you have lived, at length withdraw into a peaceful harbor. Think of how many waves you have encountered, how many storms, on the one hand, you have sustained in private life, how many, on the other, you have brought upon yourself in public life; long enough has your virtue been displayed in laborious and unceasing proofs – try how it will behave in leisure. The greater part of your life, certainly the better part of it, has been given to the state; take now some part of your time for yourself as well."*
> **– Seneca.**

Here are the words of a wise man and philosopher, Seneca, found in his book **On the Shortness of Life and On the Happy Life**. He knew the importance of a pause. He noticed how life needs constant checks and balances to make sure that we are aligned with our goals. He, himself, spent some time alone to pause and assess his progress. With such a pause, he lived a fulfilled life. As a result, he is a world-renowned philosopher and author too. It just goes to show that you need to seclude yourself from the world and its noise often to see how much distance you have covered in your journey towards realizing your dreams. Life without self-examination and evaluation is useless.

PAUSE

Now I want to introduce you to PAUSE as an acronym:

P: Presence
A: Affirmations (Self-talk)
U: Uniqueness
S: Scholar
E: Endurance

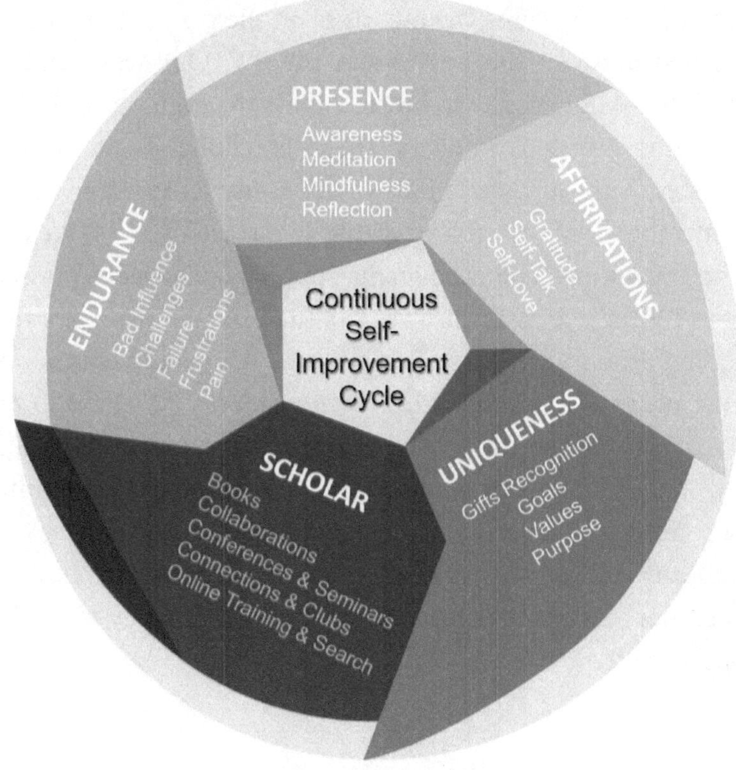

Figure 2 – Contrninuous Self-Improvement Cycle

To get a thorough understanding of the elements of PAUSE shown in Figure 2 above, here below is a detailed explanation of each one for your enlightenment:

P: Presence

In the world we live in today, a lot is happening that distracts our attention. We are bombarded with all sorts of demands from friends and family, work and church, and finally our smartphones and TVs. We are home and want to watch TV; we don't watch one channel for long and end up flipping through various channels. Meanwhile, our smartphone keeps beeping with notifications from various social media sites, and we leave the TV remote control by our side to start checking the messages on the phone. Our attention is switched between the phone and the TV. Our wife sends our daughter to ask for money to buy relish for the evening, and we end up telling her we don't know what she is talking about. Why? We never listen with our hearts but we are ready to hear and respond promptly, therefore, we end up giving incorrect answers. We are so absorbed by the messages on our smartphones and whatever program is on the TV that we easily lose track of the real and important things happening around us. Blaise Pascal said, *"All man's miseries derive from not being able to sit quietly in a room alone."* We have lost that element of paying attention to our actions and our surrounding. This leads us to take things for granted and our failure to lead a fulfilled life. Secondly, as a result of not paying attention to our actions or our surroundings we remain clueless. "A lack of **attention direction** is a real disorder," emphasizes Grandmaster Kevin Horsley in his book [emphasis added].

How can we bring sanity back to our lives? Grandmaster Kevin Horsley informs us that we have to sharpen up our intellect by returning to the habit of doing one thing at a time. "Rediscover the value of consecutive tasking, instead of settling for the quality dilution associated with simultaneous tasking. Exceptional work is always associated with periods of deep concentration," he further says. We must move away from multi-tasking to doing one task at a time, by so doing, we shall reclaim our productivity.

Apart from doing one task at a time, we must learn to find time for reflection to get back our concentration. Reflection is looking back at the day and seeing how we have performed. Through reflection, we look at all the tasks we had planned for the day, whether we have done all of them or not, and how we performed them; whether excellently or badly. We also consider areas we are good at and those we need some improvement in. Sparing ourselves ten to fifteen minutes every evening before we go to bed will help us greatly to get back our attention. We shall get back in the zone through reflection.

Then, we also need to set time aside twice or thrice a week, even every day, for meditation early in the morning or any time of the day, and before we go to bed at night. We need to train our minds to stay focused on one thing like breathing. Meditation although new to most parts of the world has been a common practice to many people from the East and in some religions such as Christianity and Buddhism.

We can start meditation by first learning to control the way we breathe, paying attention to the breath only while ignoring anything happening in the background. You can learn meditation from YouTube where every beginner interested in meditation is taken through the breathing awareness technique. This helps you to pause the mind and teach it to be present. The focus on your breathing brings back your power of concentration. Once you regain your power of concentration, you find yourself on the road to greatness. Challenge yourself today and learn how to meditate. Then let meditation be your daily morning practice to bring yourself back in the zone. With a clear mind, you shall be in a position to plan your day and be able to achieve your daily goals by paying attention to each one. With a clear mind, you find yourself being aware of the changes taking place in your environment. Being knowledgeable of the changes will then propel you to take the necessary actions that will urge you to attain your goals. Now that you are aware of the importance of meditation. I urge you to go to YouTube and search for meditation lessons for beginners.

In addition to the above, exercise helps us to regain our concentration. Bear in mind that every time you and I accomplish any task, we lose our energy and our sense of focus. To bring back that focus, we must work out or take a walk every day. Imagine yourself tired and just knocked off from work leaving some projects unfinished. What happens? If you are like me, those unfinished projects keep bombarding my mind. As a result, I become more tired, and as my mind is still busy finding ways to accomplish those projects, I find myself having sleepless nights. To refresh my mind and stay focused, I always make sure that I hit the gym thrice a week. With working out, or taking a casual walk in the evening, we kill two birds with one stone. Why? We strengthen both our physical and mental stamina. If you have been lazy and have been putting off working out, this is the moment you need to think twice about it.

Finally, you can regain your attention through visualization. Do you know that the mind works through pictures? Whatever you see with the minds' eye, you easily accomplish. Most athletes and footballers, to win their games, had to close themselves in a room, sit quietly and envision themselves playing that game several times in their minds before the day of playing the actual game. Having had time to envision themselves vividly playing the game and winning it in their minds, they end up scoring points on the actual game day. Learning from them, we too can spare time to see ourselves accomplishing great works through visualization. It might be a new concept to some of us, but that does not make it difficult. Whatever we do now, was once very difficult in the beginning, messy in the middle and smooth at the end. Practice makes permanent, so let's keep repeating it until it becomes part of us.

A: Affirmations (Self-talk)

> *"Mind is the Master power that moulds and makes,*
> *and Man is Mind, and evermore he takes the Tool of*
> *Thought, and, shaping what he wills, Brings forth a*
> *thousand joys, a thousand ills: He thinks in secret,*
> *and it comes to pass: Environment is but his looking-*
> *glass."*
> **- James Allen**

In his book titled, **As A Man Thinketh**, James Allen stated that "As a man thinketh in his heart so is he." His thoughts not only embrace the whole of a man's being but are so comprehensive as to reach out to every condition and circumstance of his life. A man is literally what he thinks, his character being the complete sum of all his thoughts.

We become what we think most often. If we think negatively of ourselves, we reap the fruits of our negativity; and if we engage our mind in positive thoughts and positive self-talk, we reap the fruits of our positivity. Hence, we become what we most often think about. Many times, we have engaged ourselves in negative self-talk. Before I dive deep into self-talk, let me define what it is. Simply put, self-talk is whatever we say when we talk to ourselves. Whatever we say to ourselves all the time, gets stuck in our subconscious mind. Dr. Shad Helmestetter (Ph.D.) states in his book titled **What to Say When You Talk to Your Self,** that because the subconscious mind does not know what is true and what is not, in time it will accept what you are telling it and act on it. We frequently say to ourselves, "I can't… It's difficult… No, I am not capable of…" and many other similar negative statements. We harbor what Joyce Meyer in her book called, **Battlefield of the Mind: Winning the Battle in Your Mind**, calls wilderness mentalities. Whenever we say such statements to ourselves, we are affirming that that's the way we see ourselves. In the end, what happens? Any negative statement we make about ourselves soon comes to pass. You must be careful with the negative statements that frequently come out of your mouth. These statements have the power to shape and mold you.

We can grow and lead a life of greatness the moment we change our self-talk. The affirmations we say to ourselves over time become true. These are called *self-fulfilling prophecies.* Have you not achieved something great after telling yourself that you are great, that you are born a winner, and are relentless? Haven't you passed a difficult examination, having told yourself that you can easily pass any examination? Why then having tasted greatness do we resort to our negativity? Engaging ourselves in positive self-talk all the time makes us become whatever we desire to be. We must, therefore, learn to engage our minds in positive self-talk. Here are examples of affirmations you can learn from to help develop your own; I have taken them from the book titled **What to Say When You Talk to Your Self** by Dr. Shad Helmestetter (Ph.D.):

I always do everything I need to do when I need to do it.
I never argue or let my emotions work against me.
I have a good memory. I easily and automatically
remember any name or anything that is important to me.
I eat only what I should.
I am a good listener - I hear everything that is said. I am
attentive, interested, and aware of everything that is
going on around me.
I have the courage to state my opinions. I take
responsibility for myself and everything I say and do.
I never spend more than I earn. I am financially
responsible, both for my present and for my future.
I set goals and I follow them. I set my sights, take the
appropriate action, and achieve my goals.
I spend time with my family and my loved ones. I enjoy
sharing their lives with mine and my life with theirs.

Just imagine yourself saying such affirmations to yourself every day. Would you be filled with positive or negative energy? If you do not want to or cannot write your own affirmations, you could always listen to and repeat the affirmations found on YouTube. Remember, this is all in an effort to change your life because ultimately you have the power inside you to change it.

U: Uniqueness

How often have you had time to understand and appreciate your uniqueness? You might not have had the time or you might say you don't have time to do that. Yet you have a lot of time to entertain your friends. Why not set aside time to entertain yourself? Why not take the time to learn about what you are made up of? Why not take the time to understand your strengths and weaknesses, your joys and worries? Discovering yourself is one of the most important requirements for becoming yourself.

There are innumerable ways through which a person can discover themselves. Below are some of them:

- **Self-introspection**: looking at yourself and listening to your deepest desires and wishes. Introspection is the examination of one's conscious thoughts and feelings. Introspection generally provides privileged access to one's mental states, not mediated by other sources of knowledge, so that the individual experience of the mind is unique. Introspection can determine any number of mental states including: sensory, bodily, cognitive, emotional, and so forth.

  Introspection means looking inward, examining your ideas, thoughts, and feelings. Self-introspection/self-observation is important as it is a kind of regular check on self-development which helps you to know what you have achieved so far. Talk to yourself and ask yourself questions.

On her website, PositivePsychology.com (https://positive-psychology.com/introspection-self-reflection/), Courtney E Ackerman suggests the following questions that one can use for your self-introspection:

1. Am I using my time wisely?
2. Am I taking anything for granted?
3. Am I employing a healthy perspective?
4. Am I living true to myself?
5. Am I waking up in the morning ready to take on the day?
6. Am I thinking negative thoughts before I fall asleep?
7. Am I putting enough effort into my relationships?
8. Am I taking care of myself physically?

9. Am I letting matters that are out of my control stress me out?

10. Am I achieving the goals that I've set for myself?

According to Sara Uzer, some of the benefits of self-introspection are that it allows you to notice negative patterns in your life; it keeps you focused on the bigger picture; it prevents you from worrying about things out of your control; it helps you face your fears; it allows you to clearly define happiness on your terms and it allows you to make decisions based on your conscience.

- **Feedback from others:** people you adequately interact with may help you understand yourself in areas that you are blind to. Sometimes the people may not necessarily point out something new about yourself but only confirm you in your weakness or strength.

- **Events of necessity:** just as they say that 'necessity is the mother of invention,' circumstances of great need may bring out our qualities that we would otherwise have not discovered under normal circumstances. For instance, under normal circumstances, you may not have known that you can run very fast until you are chased by something.

- **Inspiration/Modeling:** other people who have successfully discovered and embraced themselves become a source of inspiration and motivation for self-discovery. As they express their true selves, your "self" starts moving inside you. Modeling implies a situation whereby a person identifies role models (including coaches and mentors) from whom to learn by imitation alone, without any specific verbal direction by the therapist and a general process in which persons serve as models for others, exhibiting the behavior worthy to be imitated by the others. John C. Maxwell says that "most people who decide to grow personally find their first mentors in the pages of books."

- **Journaling:** journaling involves writing down all your daily thoughts in a diary or notebook. Wake up early in the morning and start writing anything you are grateful for on that particular day. Also remember to write down your concerns or worries about that particular day. Over time you shall get to know where your thoughts dwell the most: a trend. This trend will assist you to make necessary adjustments in your life that will eventually lead you to excellence. You can then learn to set up your personal goals through this process of journaling. And these goals will lead you to live a purposeful life. What a beautiful way of leaving an impact in this world.

- **Career Guidance:** professional carrier guides can help you to discover yourself through the application of various psycho-spiritual exercises. Career guidance is the guidance given to individuals to help them acquire the knowledge, information, skills, and experience necessary to identify career options.

- **SWOT Analysis:** SWOT stands for strengths, weaknesses, opportunities, and threats and it is a strategic planning technique used to help a person or organization identify strengths, weaknesses, opportunities, and threats related to business competition or project planning. You can conduct your self-analysis using this method as well especially in looking at your weaknesses and strengths to understand self.

S: Scholar

Knowing your capabilities and deficiencies and having understood the changes in the environment by realizing your purpose through coming face to face with yourself, you can now decide what course of action to take.

Self-improvement is another requirement for remaining relevant in the changing environment. The changes in our environment pose great challenges to some of the skills that we acquired a long time ago. With the advancement of technology, I have seen a lot of people losing their jobs. Machines and robots have declared most people redundant and have taken over some people's jobs. This prompts me to ask you the question: what are you doing to remain competitive and relevant? If you are still sleeping now, surely you should not be surprised when you shall have a rude awakening later. Most people who have been laid off because of the changes in the world are now frustrated. Some have committed suicide because they felt that they could not cope with their current status.

Become your own boss by educating yourself and by becoming a continuous learner. You can do this by looking around to see the current trends and finding out the skills that will be most relevant to a change in the environment.

Knowing your strengths and weaknesses can allow you to know the skills you need to remain valuable in this world. Take up a course online, teach yourself some new skills, and become one of the great people of our time. There are a lot of new courses online that cater for the challenges posed by the advancement of various technologies. Search for the new skills, learn them, and master them, and you shall be the master of your own game.

Do not be tempted to say that you are too old to learn. You are capable of learning and understanding anything new. Remember that it all begins with your thoughts. If you tell yourself you are invincible, you shall conquer mountains. However, the moment you tell yourself you are too old to learn new skills, you are in for it. You will indeed struggle to learn. I want to encourage you to constantly learn, broaden your thinking, and claim your place in this challenging world. Be a scholar; a great scholar is willing to learn all the time. You are special, you are unique, so never settle for less. Take that bold step now to choose a new course with the skills you need to remain relevant. John C. Maxwell observes that "growth stops when you lose the tension between where you are and where you could be."

E: Endurance

Finally, once you embark on this course of life, be assured that there are obstacles you shall come across. Either you step over them or you stumble. It's a tough choice you have to make. It needs strong people to make it to the end, and people who are willing to follow *the road less traveled*. New life comes with its challenges; these challenges are the great opportunities that prepare you to make it. Are you ready and willing to take up these challenges? Are you strong enough to overcome the urge to withdraw? It will never be easy. You shall lose some of your friends along the way. Others will call you mad and insane. Will you stick to your guns?

Dozens of people have accomplished much by choosing a new path to follow while others stumbled and got discouraged along the way. You are called for greatness. With your head held high and a spring in your step, walk tall towards your destination. Ignore all those people who won't believe in you, those who won't believe the course of life you have chosen. Without ever betraying the profound and all-time African wisdom that says *'kalikokha nkanyama, tili tiwiri ntianthu'* (Chewa) or *'umuntu ngumuntu, ngabantu'* (Zulu), only you matter the most in as far as the determination and the commitment to personal development is concerned. Only you matter the most.

Endure the name-calling, the misunderstandings, insults, and discouragements from friends and family. Endure the pain of missing out on those moments you could have spent with your friends having fun. It's only when you discipline yourself and focus on the new journey that you shall get there. Be resilient and relentless. Look inside yourself for the will power to reach your destiny.

Through pausing, you can deal with obstacles better. You are able to endure because you can take the time to re-energize and re-focus yourself. As a result, you will awaken the giant within and endure the obstacles brought to you time and time again. So, take time to pause and reflect on your life and priorities, to be able to overcome the obstacles that will come your way.

In summary, we have learned that we can get our attention or concentration back by applying the PAUSE strategy. With a pause, both you and I can unleash the giant lying within us. With this giant awakened, we are assured of excellence and living our dream life. We must learn to pay attention to our actions and surroundings; check whatever we say to ourselves when alone; understand that we are unique and meant to achieve greatness with this uniqueness; engage in continuous self-improvement through self-learning or personal initiative; and endure the pain of losing friends in the process, so that we can live our life in full. You are in control, so change the game plan now to realize your dream. The responsibility for you to become the best version of yourself is in your hands.

In the next and final chapter, I shall take the opportunity to remind you of the most vital concepts we have covered in this book as your takeaway for you to excel in life. I believe that during our journey together you have learned some ideas that, once implemented, will reveal the original version of yourself and will help you to become the architect and author of your destiny. Turn to the next page for reminders of what we have covered thus far.

Chapter Ten

TAKE THE TIME TO FIND YOU AMIDST CHAOS

"Change isn't just one thing, just one time, just one big revelation. Change occurs in stages, and phases, which each add depth, color, character, and create a multidimensional, multifaceted you."
– Doe Zantamata

To be what you truly want to be in life, to live your dream life, you need to find yourself a purpose. Have you found yours? Remember, you and I need a compelling purpose to pursue, to live our life to the full. It is when you tend to be a purpose-driven person that you are then ready and geared to face any adversity or challenge squarely in the face, from the right perspective, attitude, and with the right scale of values. Find one at all costs. Pursue it relentlessly and with resilience. Surely, detractors, distractions, challenges, and obstacles will stand in between us and our purpose; they will try to persuade us to surrender and give up. But, if we are committed to living this dream life we will put all our attention and strength on this purpose, not becoming perturbed until we realize that dream.

Appreciating the child in us and getting back to him/her time and again will allow us to live our life to the full. Never banish the curiosity of the child inside you. This child asks questions that, as grown-ups, we feel and think do not make sense, but in actual fact are great, and make a lot of sense if we find time to think them through. Nourish the questions that flow from the child within. With him/her in the lead, we are headed for greatness. Live your purpose by learning to nurture the child inside you.

To live any type of life we dream of, it requires us to change the way we have been doing things. Remember that it is insanity to do the same things again and again expecting different results. We will only see change the moment you and I learn to do things differently. From my understanding, for each one of us to acquire and gain something new, we must go through a process called **OLA** (observe or see, learn or judge and apply or act). We use our eyes to take pictures of whatever is happening around us and store these pictures in our subconscious mind. The more we **observe**, the better we become at absorbing the new changes in the environment we live in. Then we capture our observations on either paper, in notebooks and notepads, or on our smartphones, laptops, and personal computers. We then take our time to learn new strategies of combating the changes for us to remain game-changers. We do this by reading and recalling until it sticks in our minds. As we do this, we **learn** this knowledge and skill. Finally, we recall and put into practice whatever we have acquired through observation and learning.. We **apply** this new knowledge and skill to assist us in overcoming the challenges brought about by the changes.

Tempus fugit. This is a Latin proverb implying that time flies. How are we managing our time? If you and I are not frugal with our time, we shall find ourselves with our mouth agape, wondering where the time has gone. We shall find ourselves with empty hands and yet a full year, and even decades, have passed. Remember time is money and we are to use it wisely, guarding it jealously at all costs. Saint Mother Theresa of Calcutta observed that "Life is short but enough for those who live it well." Time is the only resource you can never get back once it's lost. Use it to achieve your dreams and live the life you want. Start planning your day's activities in advance. You are the master of your game. In **Striking Thoughts: Bruce Lee's Wisdom for Daily Living**, Bruce Lee advises that "If you love life, don't waste time, for time is what life is made up of."

Ever wondered why some people do very well compared to others? And having seen that there are people who are successful while others are living in dire poverty, have you ever asked yourself why this is the case? Those who are enjoying life have learned to value themselves. They know themselves well. These people have values in life and live by those values. However, if you ask the poor why they are the way they are, the obvious answer will be to blame their parents or someone else. Values don't ring a bell in their ears. If you want to live life to the full, learn to value yourself, and have values that can assist you to reach your dream life. Remember, that it's not where you are coming from that matters most, but where you are going. Lupita Nyong'o once said, "Your birthplace is not your destiny."

It is fascinating to see how much people invest in safeguarding their computers against viruses. But, how often do we keep watch of our thoughts? Are we in constant check of our thoughts? Or do we let them wander freely in our minds? Remember, we are what we repeatedly think of. If we dwell on positive thinking most of the time, we are geared to achieve excellence, however, if we indulge in negative thoughts often, we should not be surprised if we achieve nothing in life. We must be in control of our thoughts if we are to achieve greatness. Our thoughts have an impact on our emotions, and these emotions affect our attitudes, and our attitudes affect our beliefs, where our beliefs influence our behavior. Finally, our behavior influences our habits. See this ripple effect of thoughts on our habits? Why then are we not guarding our thoughts against negativity and limiting ideas? It's imperative to control our thoughts if we are to excel in life. Let's get started TODAY for a better tomorrow.

Our minds grow and make us great thinkers and achievers the moment we engage them in questioning everything. How often do you set time aside for questioning your thinking? Your actions? Your decisions? In life, we either make it or hit a blank wall. To live a fulfilled life, we have to ask ourselves open-ended questions. These questions will lead us to discover our true selves, uncover our strengths and weaknesses, and even come across the life of our dreams. See now, without questions, you and I cannot know whether we need to improve any skill set or not. Cherish your lone moments and engage yourself in questions that will take you to another level. Being alone should not make you suffer from loneliness. Instead, embrace all your lone moments as special times for solitude that is needed for extracting your precious riches within you.

It is important to note that life revolves around decision making. How do you arrive at these decisions? Who influences your decision making? Some people make decisions on their own and believe in their gut feeling. They believe in the power within them to draw out the final decision. Others, on the other hand, cannot make any decision without the influence of other people. They mostly look down upon themselves. They only think others will help them arrive at good decisions. While input from other people is important, it is imperative that we learn to make decisions based on our final conclusions and judgment. We have to own and be responsible for our decisions. To realize growth in ourselves, we must move away from being a conformist to being a non-conformist. Challenge yourself now and see how satisfying your life will turn out to be.

Finally, in this world where everything is running at supersonic speed, we need to find moments for a pause. We need to find time when we can look back at our life, see what strides we have made, and how far short we still are. Evaluation and assessment of the progress made are indispensable on the journey towards personal growth and development. Isn't it great, to find time to cherish yourself? Your accomplishments? To dig deep into your failures and find out what caused you to fail? To uncover what needs to be done to correct or improve upon failure? Pausing is one of the most essential tools that we must use to grow ourselves. Yes, we are made to live an accomplished life, a legendary life; a life that contributes to the well-being of others, and part of attaining it is taking time to pause. Borrowing Steve R. Covey's language, we are supposed to grow from effectiveness to greatness or, in Abraham Maslow's terms, from self-actualization to transcendence.

We can make it to our desired destination when we sit down and assess our progress while monitoring our thoughts; keep improving ourselves in areas we are lacking; and constantly find time to sit down with others like mentors who can lead us to our greatness through their honest feedback. The onus is yours to survive or strive and to live or die. What will you choose?

ABOUT THE AUTHOR

Robert Salijeni is an adventurous, inquisitive, open-minded, spiritually grounded, and vivacious man who lives his life inside out. His life revolves around making decisions from his gut feeling and he possesses a spontaneous personality. He is an entrepreneur, public speaker, and trainer who manages roofhouse limited as its Chief Executive Officer, and is also one of the directors of Unlocking Your Potential, a consultancy firm specializing in the coaching, leadership and public speaking skills development, as well as mentoring of entrepreneurs, middle and senior Managers. roofhouse limited was awarded Agency of the Year twice in a row in 2014 and 2015, while Robert was awarded Marketer of the Year in 2015 by the Chartered Institute of Marketing (CIM) Malawi Group.

He is a family man who lives in Blantyre with his darling wife, Tamanda Salijeni, and four beloved children, Annie, Augustine, Angel, and Amy.

Robert is a public speaker borne of Toastmasters International and holds a Master Practitioner Certificate in Neuro-Linguistic Programming (NLP). With the NLP certification, he turned into a life coach and mentor. He is yet to be awarded the highest accolade, Distinguished Toastmaster (DTM) in public speaking and leadership skills, by Toastmasters International in the course of 2020.

He enjoys reading books, mountain biking, hiking, and spending part of his quality time with his family.

In his quality time, he mentors and coaches others into achieving their life goals and awakening their purpose.

His next move is to continue coaching and mentoring people as a Neuro-Linguistic Programming Practitioner.

If you are stuck in life and do not know what to do next, Robert is available for you to assist you to unleash your hidden dream and live a purposeful life. You can reach him via his email address – robertsalijeni@gmail.com.

He looks forward to hearing from you and until then, remember to live a life of purpose!

REFERENCES

1. A Guide to the Good Life: The Ancient Art of Stoic Joy by William B Irvine

2. The Handy Philosophy Answer Book by Naomi Zack, Ph.D

3. Philosophy 101: From Plato and Socrates to Ethics and Metaphysics, an Essential Primer on the History of Thought by Paul Kleinman

4. An Introduction to Zen Buddhism by DT Suzuki

5. Time Management by Brian Tracy

6. Eat the Frog! 21 Great Ways to Stop Procrastinating and Get More Done in Less Time by Brian Tracy

7. Reprogram Your Subconscious – 10 Secrets to Manifest Powerful Abundance in Your Life by Jamie Cole

8. Out of Your Comfort Zone, Breaking Boundaries for a Life Beyond Limits by Emma Mardlin, Ph.D

9. The Gift in You: Discovering New Life Through Gifts Hidden in Your Mind by Dr Caroline Leaf

10. 15 Invaluable Laws of Growth by John C Maxwell

11. Thumbs Up! Five Steps to Create the Life of Your Dreams by Joey Reiman

12. Sociology, 15th Edition (2013) by John J Macionis

13. Roget's 21st Century Thesaurus in Dictionary Form, 3rd Edition. The Essential Reference for Home, School, or Office, edited by Princeton Language Institute Barbara Ann Kipfer, Ph.D, Head of Lexicographer

14. What to Say When You talk to Your Self by Shad Helmestetter, Ph.D

15. As A Man Thinketh by James Allen

16. The Purpose and Power of Authority: Discovering the Power of Your Personal Domain by Myles Munroe

17. Populorum Progression (Development of Peoples) Encyclopedia by Pope Paul VI

18. Failing Forward: Turning Mistakes into Stepping Stones for Success by John C Maxwell

19. Law of Pain by John C Maxwell

20. A More Beautiful Question: The Power of Inquiry to Spark Breakthrough Ideas by Warren Berger

21. The Art of Non-Conformity – Set Your Own Rules, Live the Life You Want and Change the World by Chris Guillebeau

22. Unlimited Memory: How to Use Advanced Learning Strategies to Learn Faster, Remember More and Be More Productive by Grandmaster Kevin Horsley

23. On the Shortness of Life and On the Happy Life by Seneca

24. Battlefield of the Mind: Winning the Battle in Your Mind by Joyce Meyer

25. PositivePsychology.com (https://positivepsychology.com/introspection-self-reflection), Courtney E Ackerman

26. Striking Thoughts: Bruce Lee's Wisdom for Daily Living by Bruce Lee